Real World
Colouring Book

For Advanced Users & Adults

50 Images

**Created From Real Life Photos
For You To Colour As You Please.**

ISBN 978-0-359-82061-0
90000
9 780359 820610

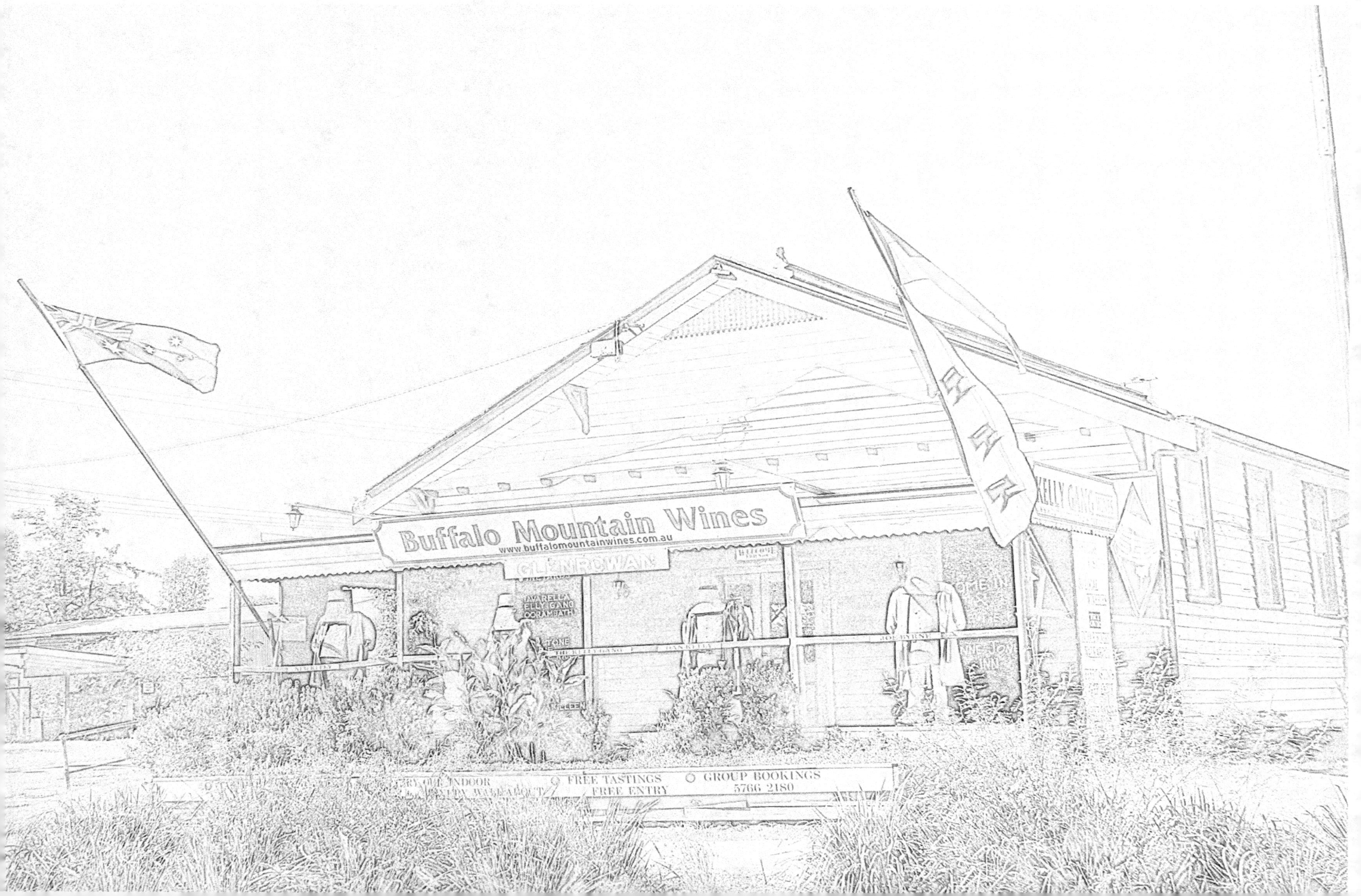
Buffalo Mountain Wines
www.buffalomountainwines.com.au
GLENROWAN
FREE TASTINGS
FREE ENTRY
GROUP BOOKINGS
5766 2180

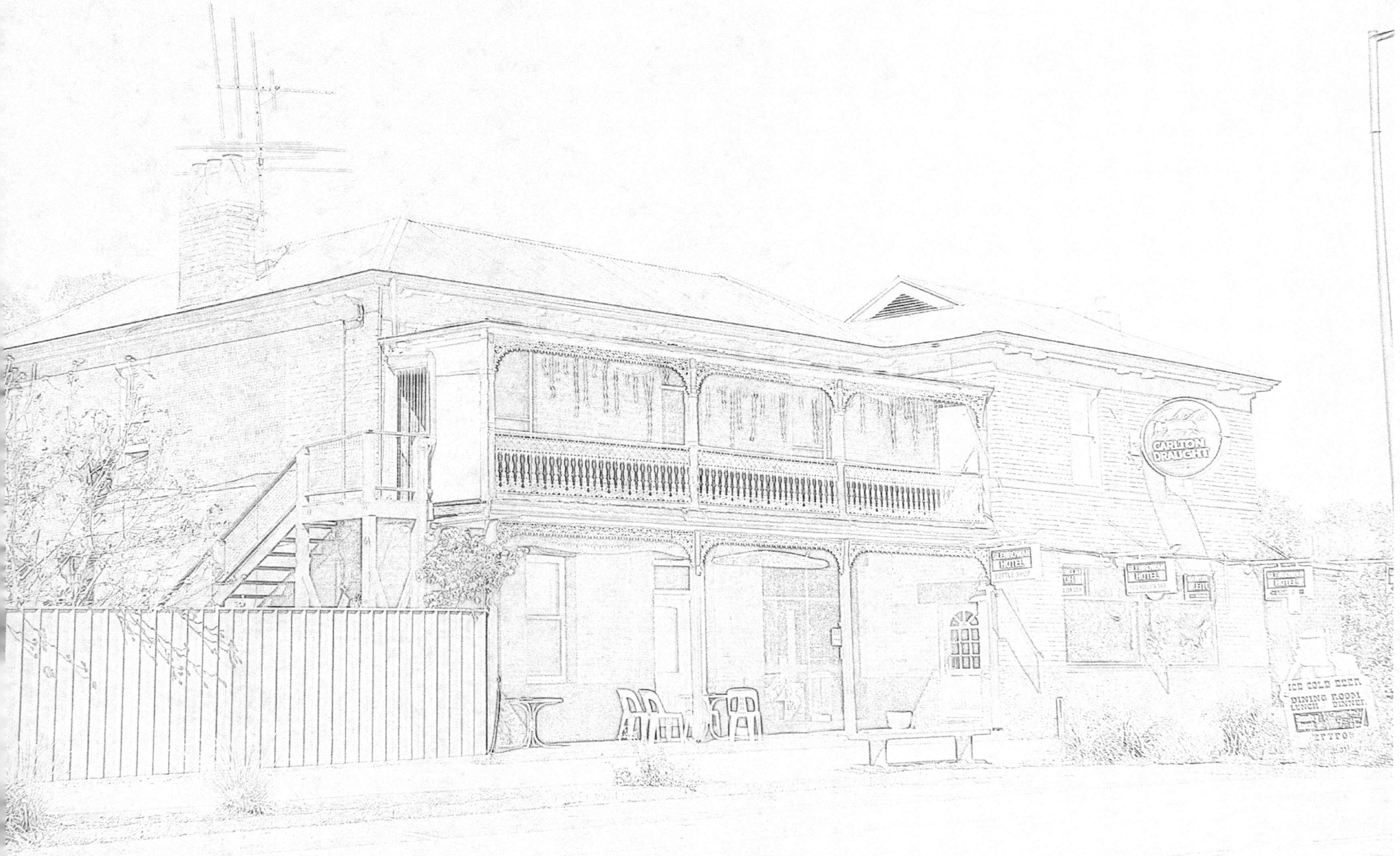

CARLTON DRAUGHT
GLENROWAN HOTEL
BOTTLE SHOP
HOTEL
HOTEL
HOTEL
ICE COLD BEER
DINING ROOM
LUNCH DINNER

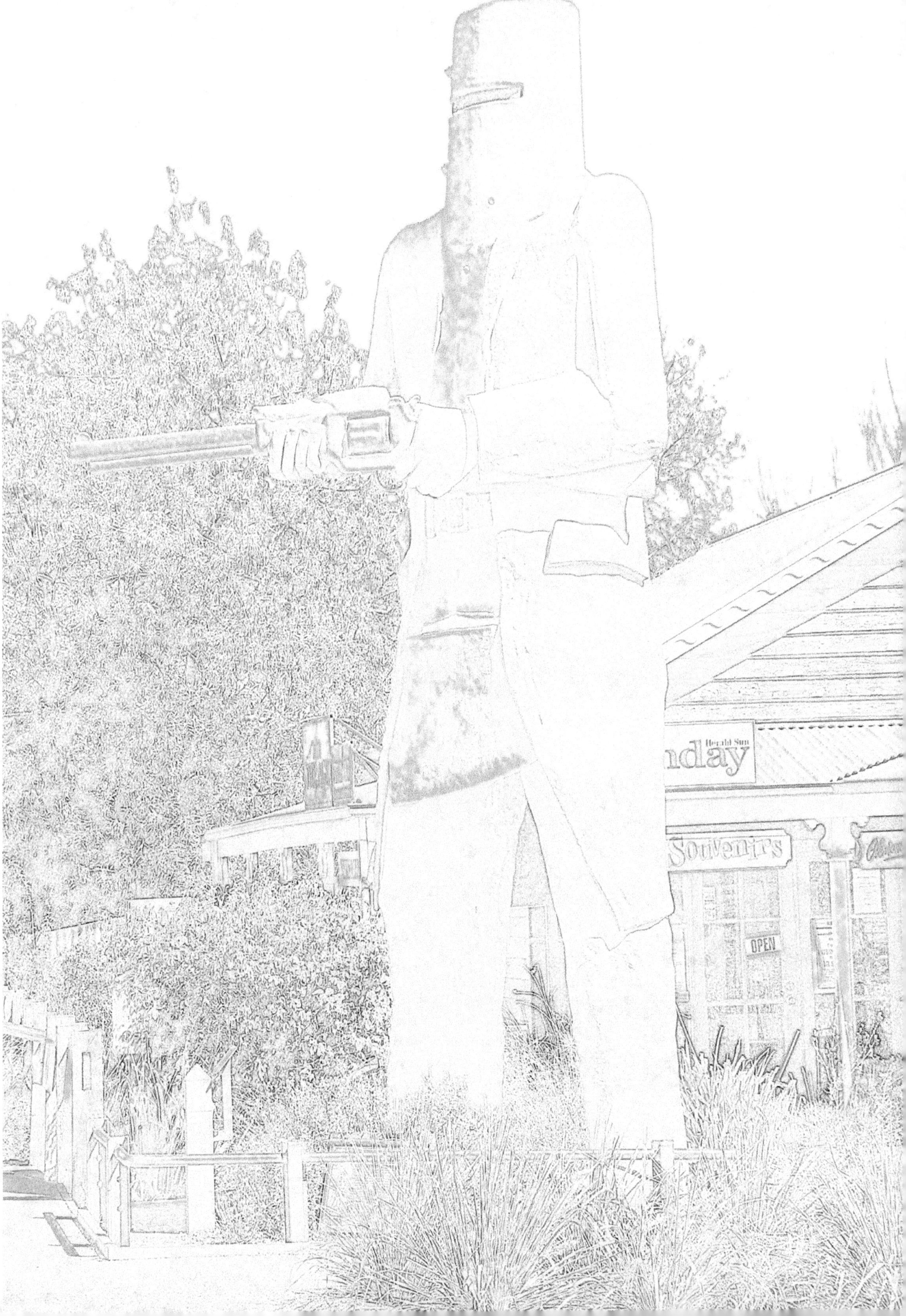
Souvenirs
OPEN

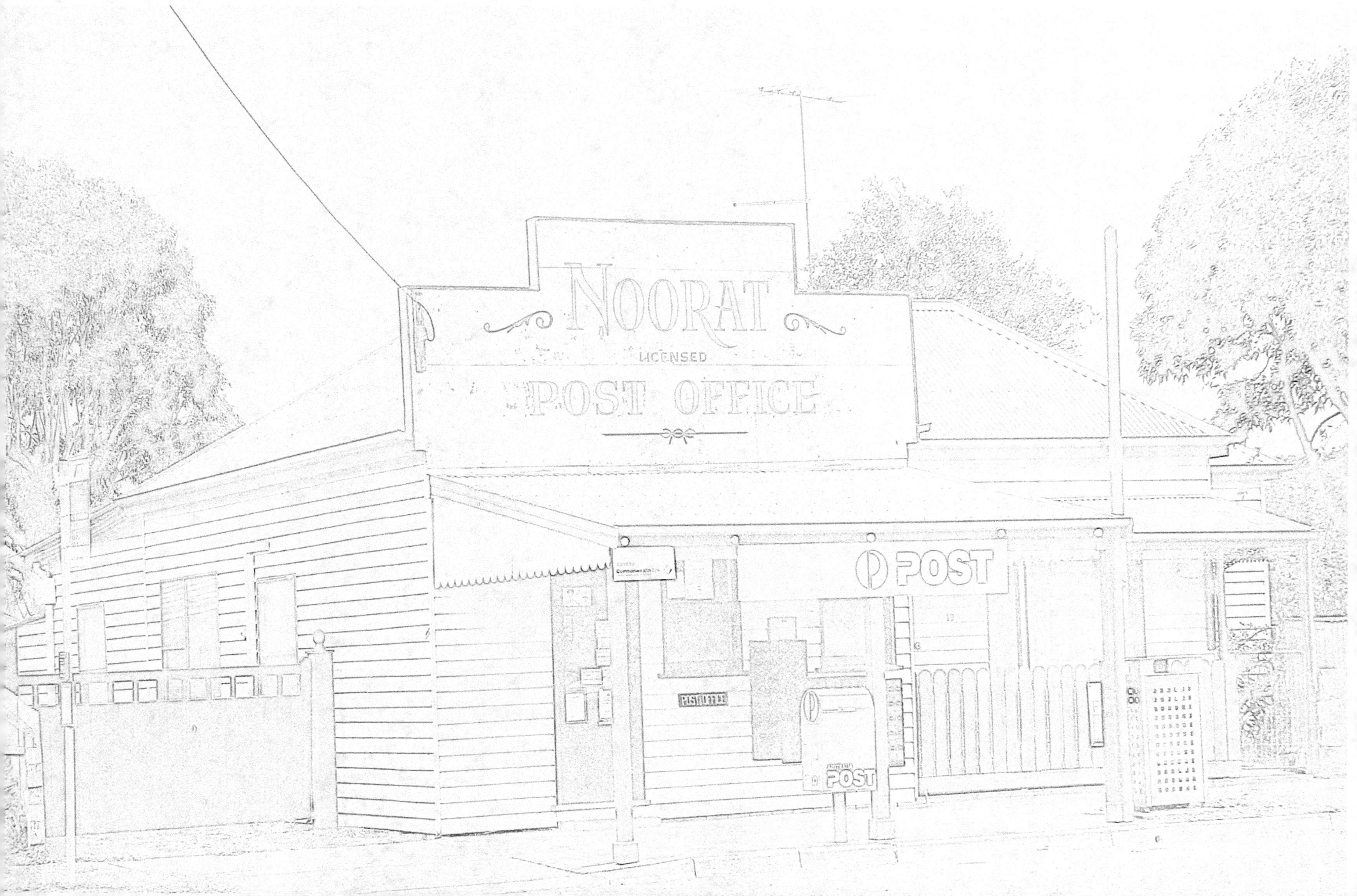
NOORAT
LICENSED
POST OFFICE
POST
POST OFFICE
POST

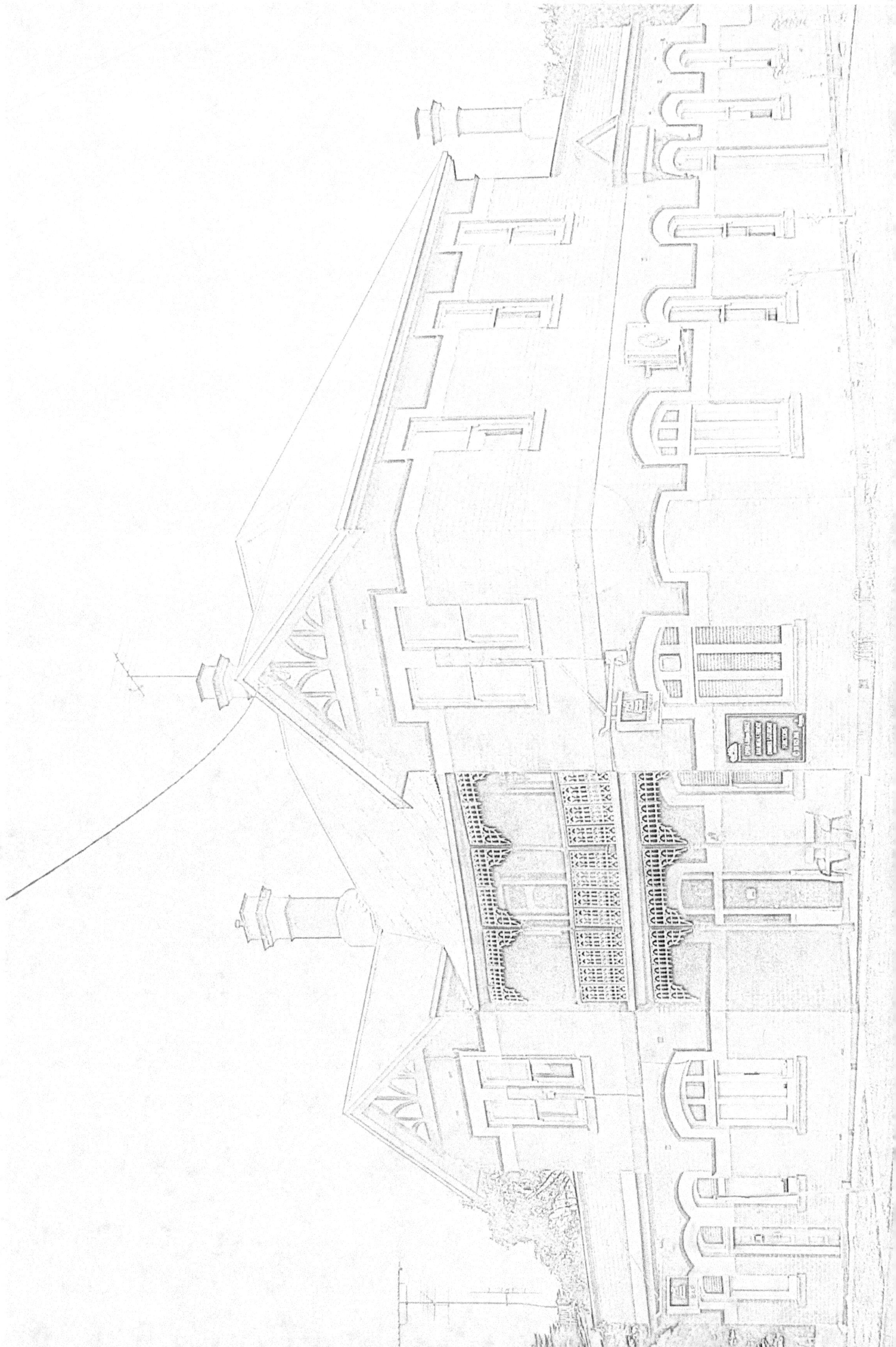

NOORAT
LICENSED
POST OFFICE
Agent for
Commonwealth Bank
POST
POST OFFICE
For Sale
AUSTRALIA
POST

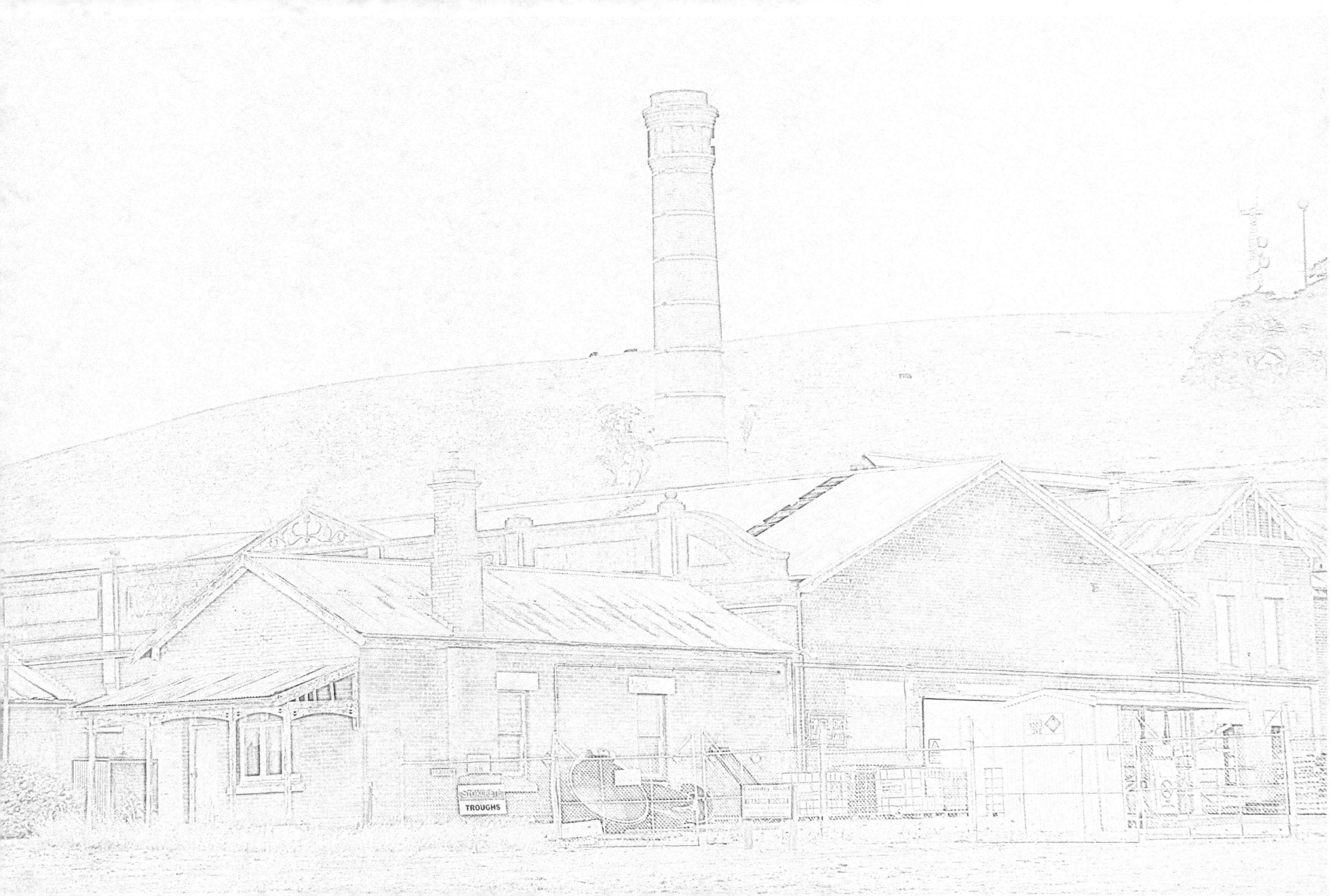
TROUGHS

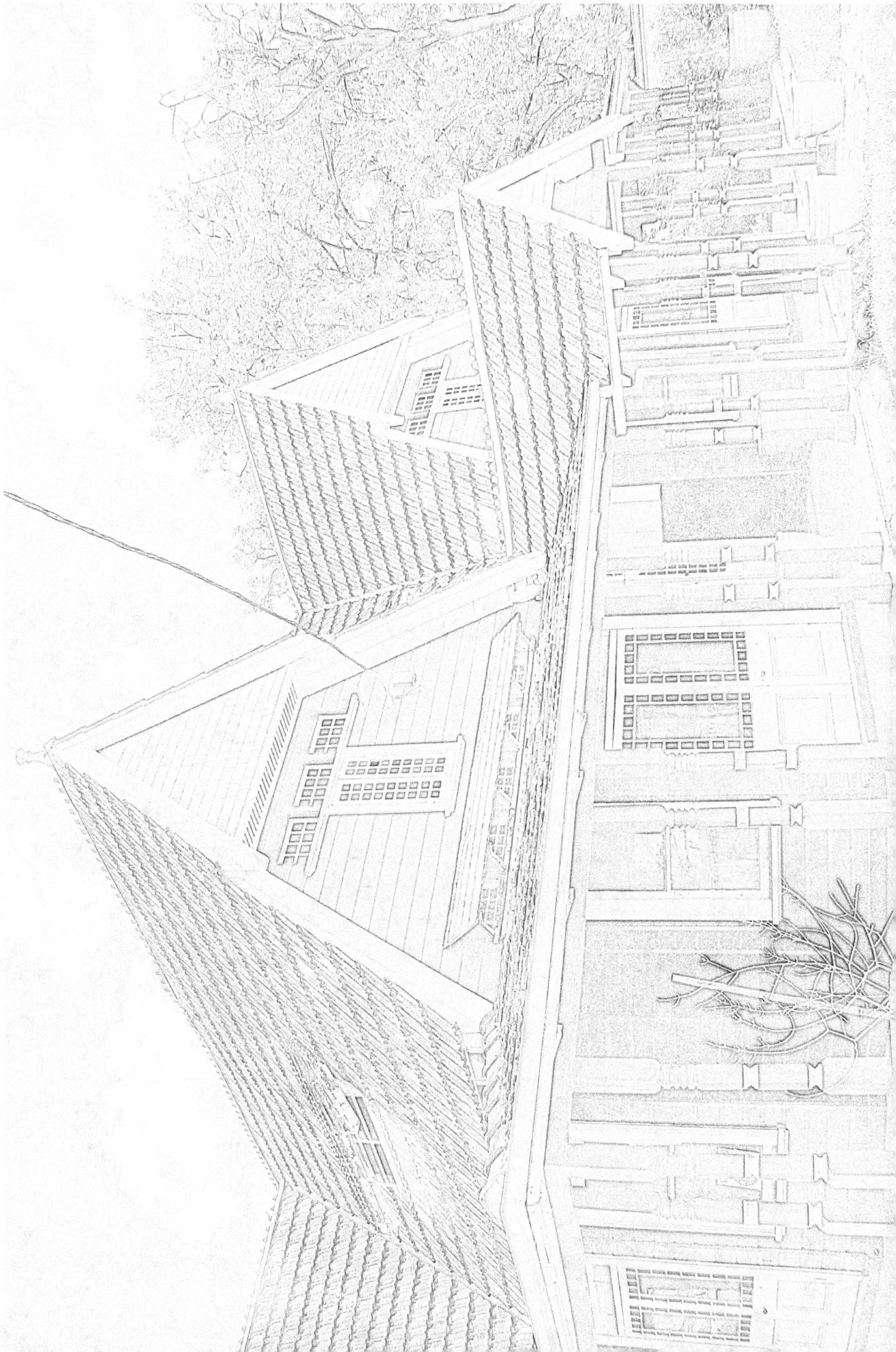

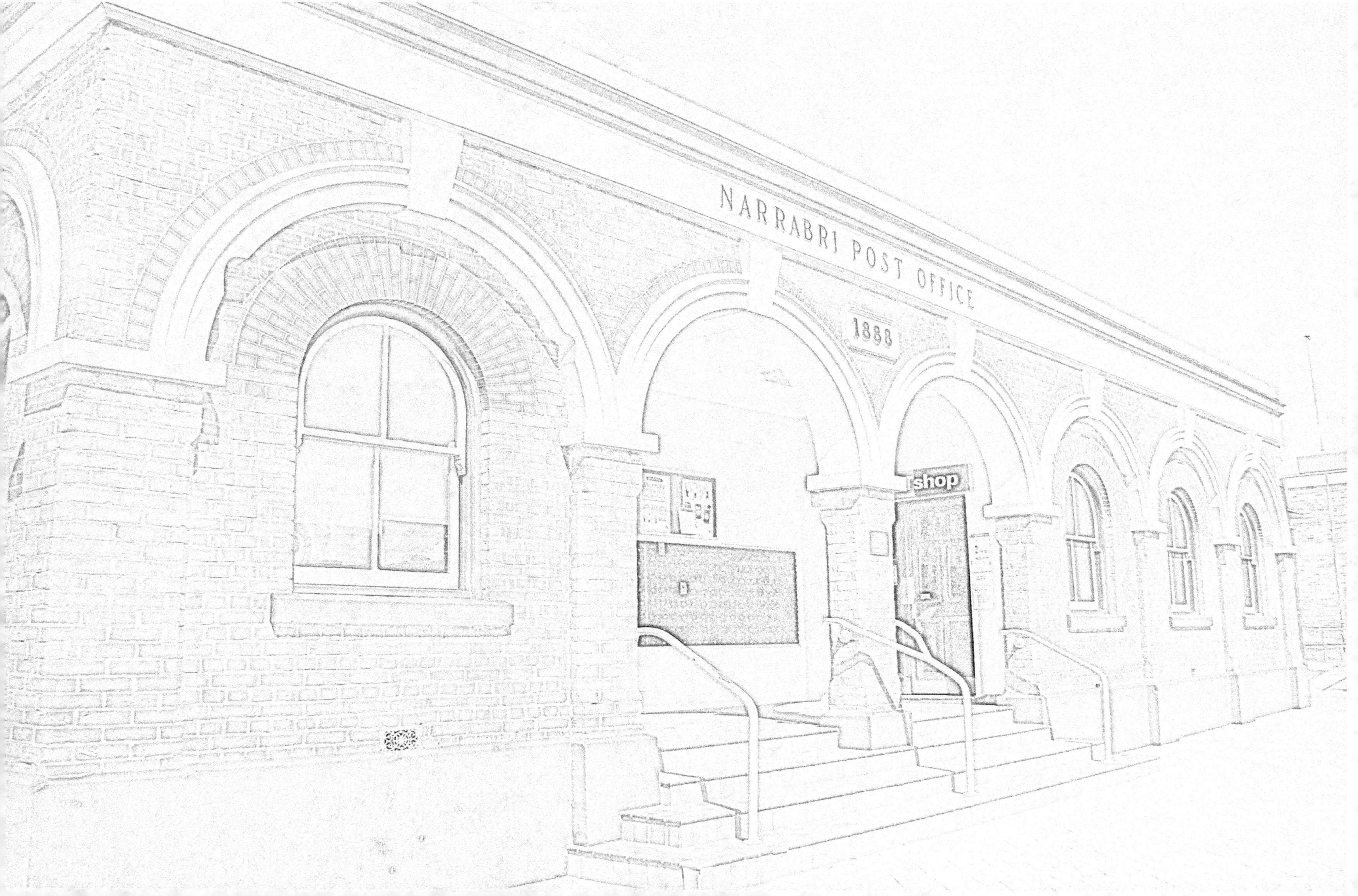
NARRABRI POST OFFICE
1888
shop

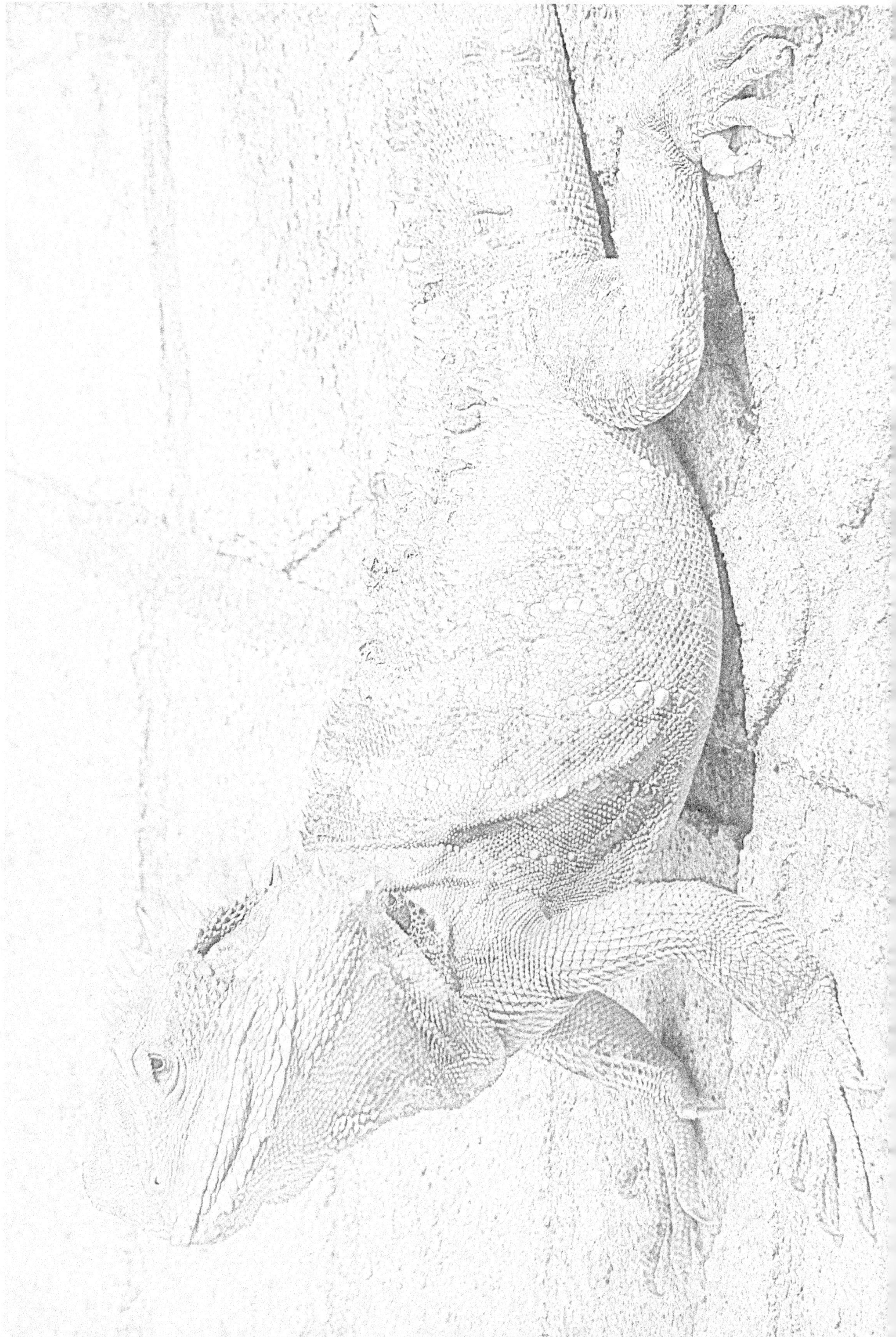

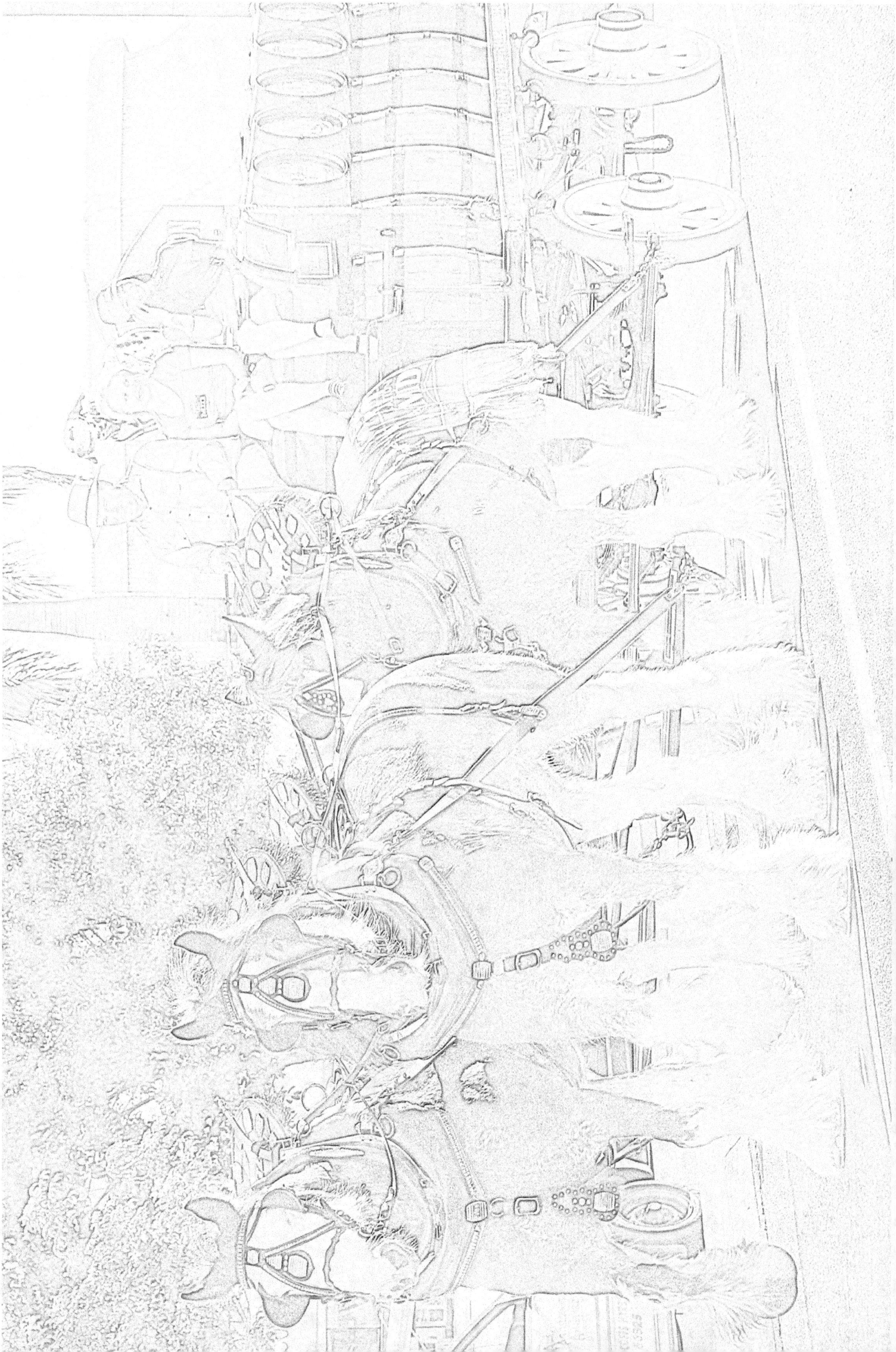

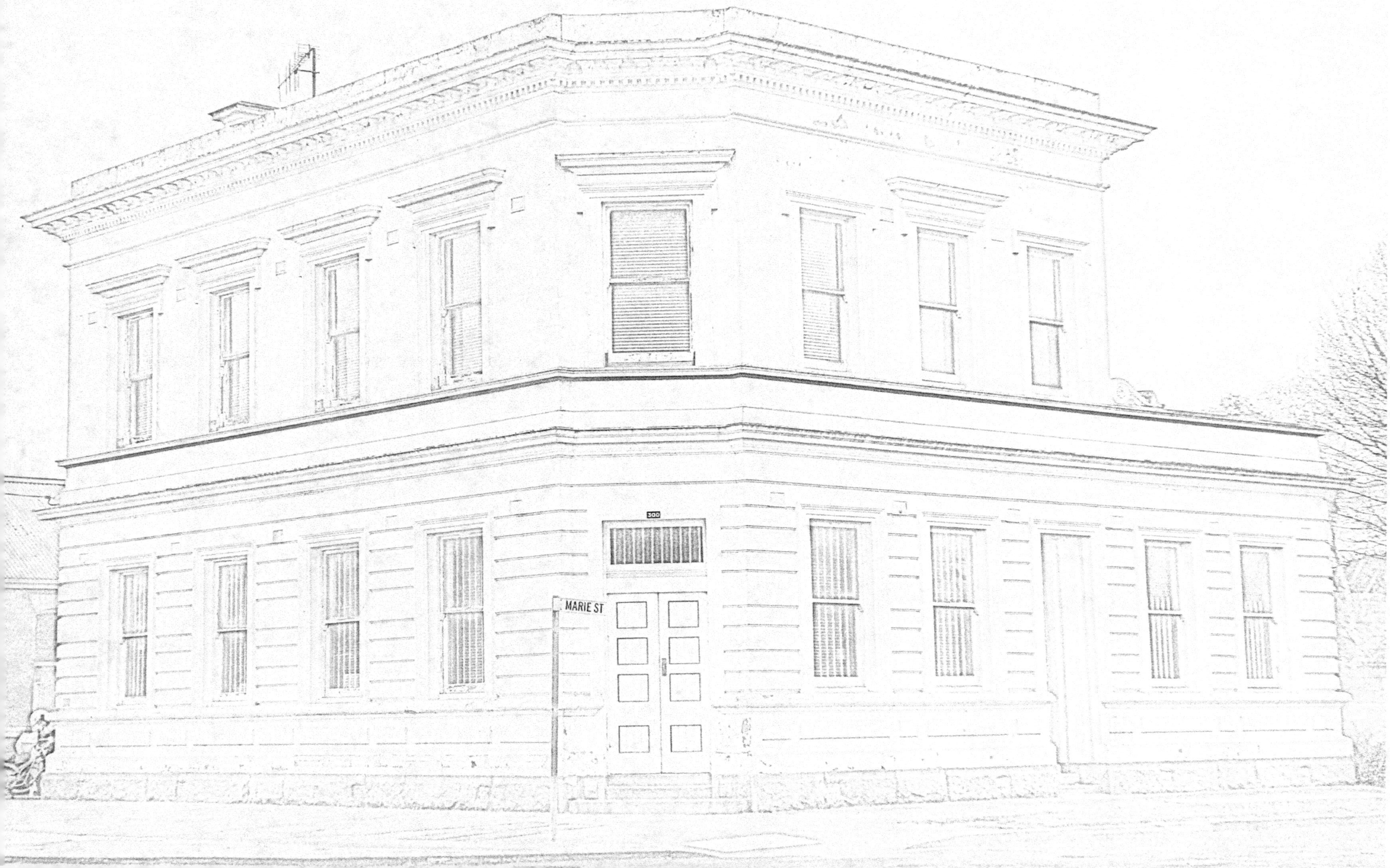
300
MARIE ST

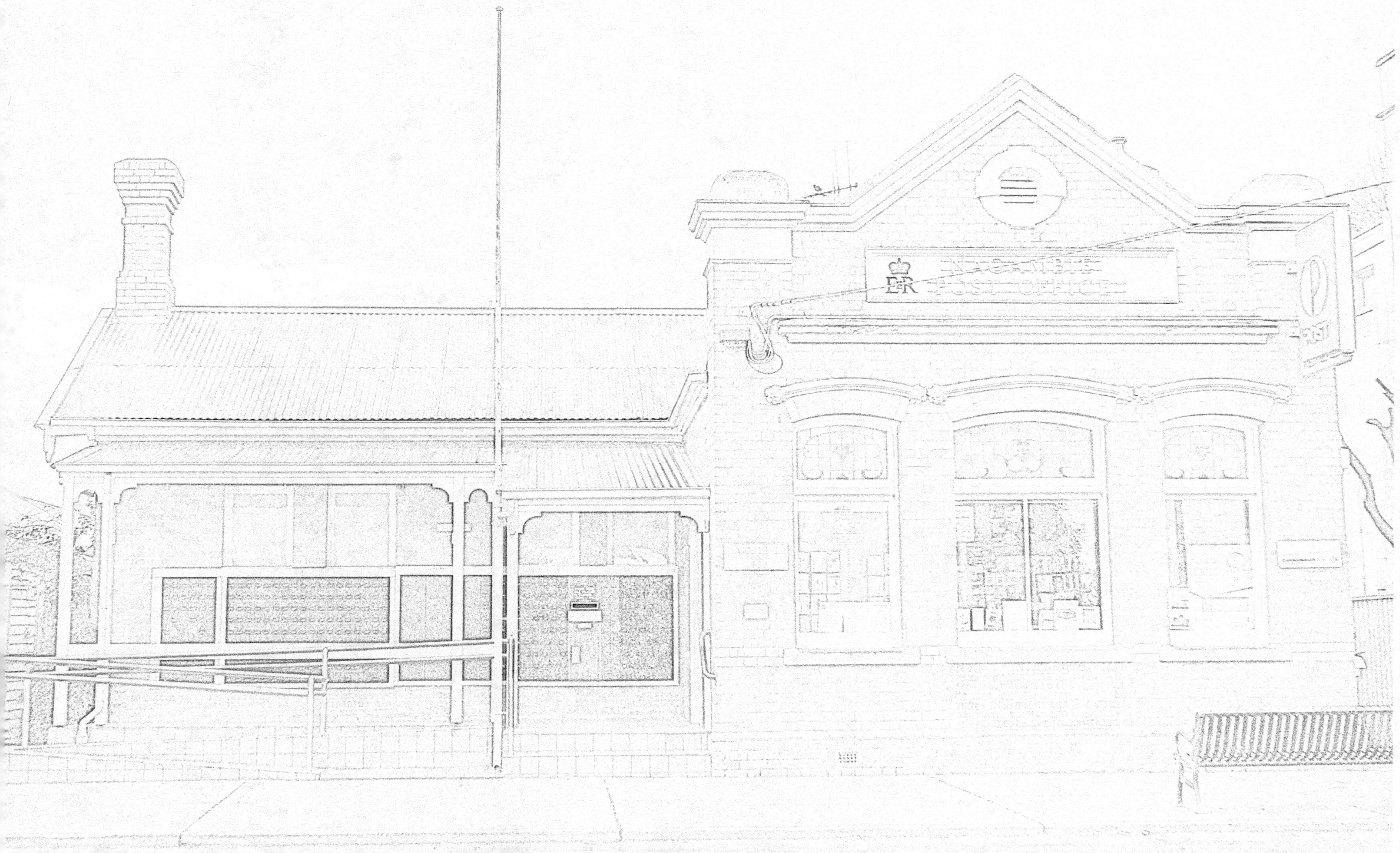
POST OFFICE

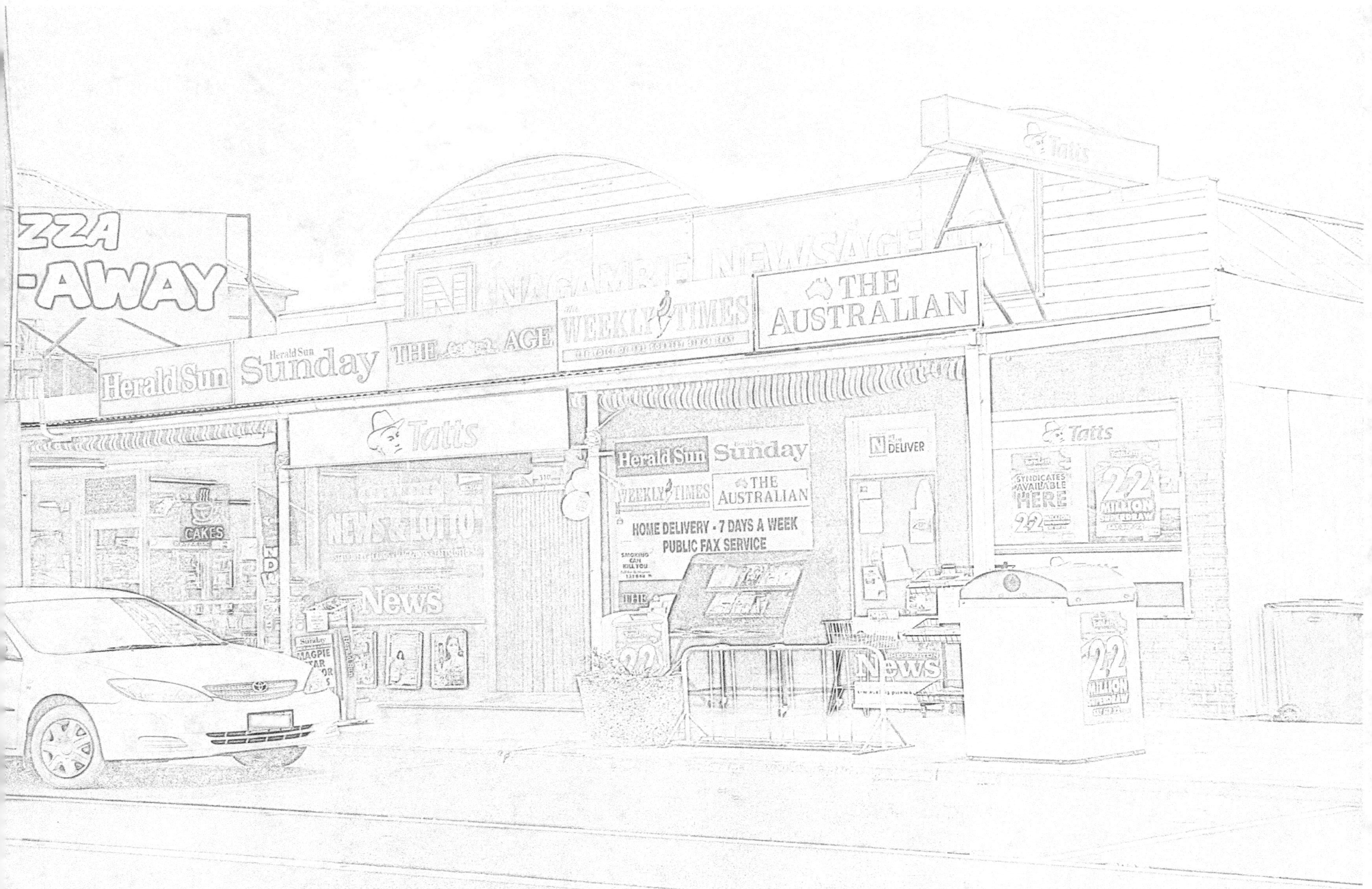
ZZA
-AWAY
Herald Sun
Herald Sun Sunday
THE AGE
the WEEKLY TIMES
THE AUSTRALIAN
NAGAMBIE NEWSAGE
Tatts
NEWS & LOTTO
News
CAKES
Herald Sun
Sunday
WEEKLY TIMES
THE AUSTRALIAN
HOME DELIVERY • 7 DAYS A WEEK
PUBLIC FAX SERVICE
SMOKING CAN KILL YOU
DELIVER
Tatts
SYNDICATES AVAILABLE HERE
22 MILLION
News

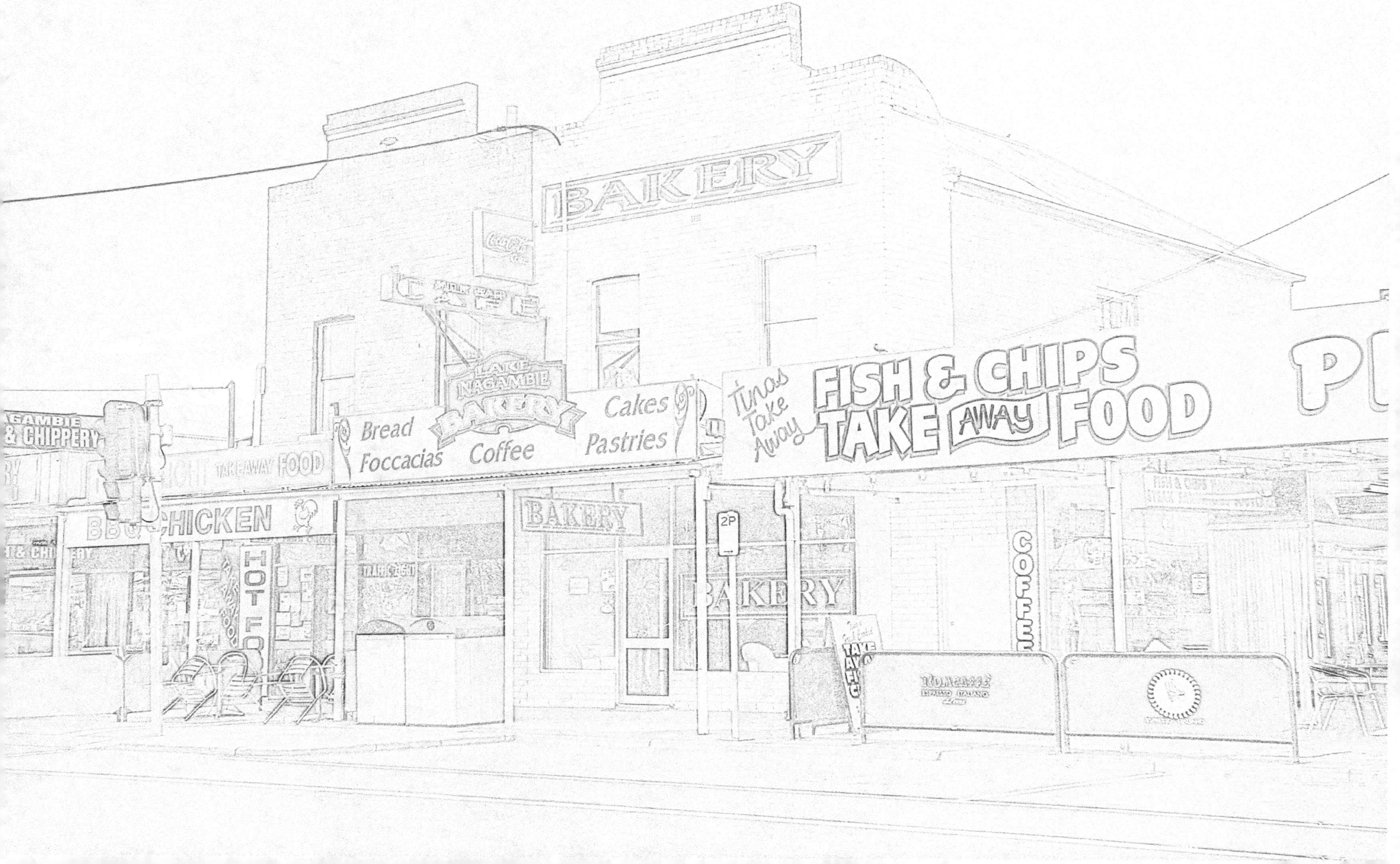
BAKERY
CAFE
LAKE NAGAMBIE BAKERY
Bread
Foccacias
Coffee
Cakes
Pastries
Tinas Take Away
FISH & CHIPS
TAKE AWAY FOOD
TAKEAWAY FOOD
BBQ CHICKEN
HOT FO
BAKERY
BAKERY
2P
COFFEE
& CHIPPERY

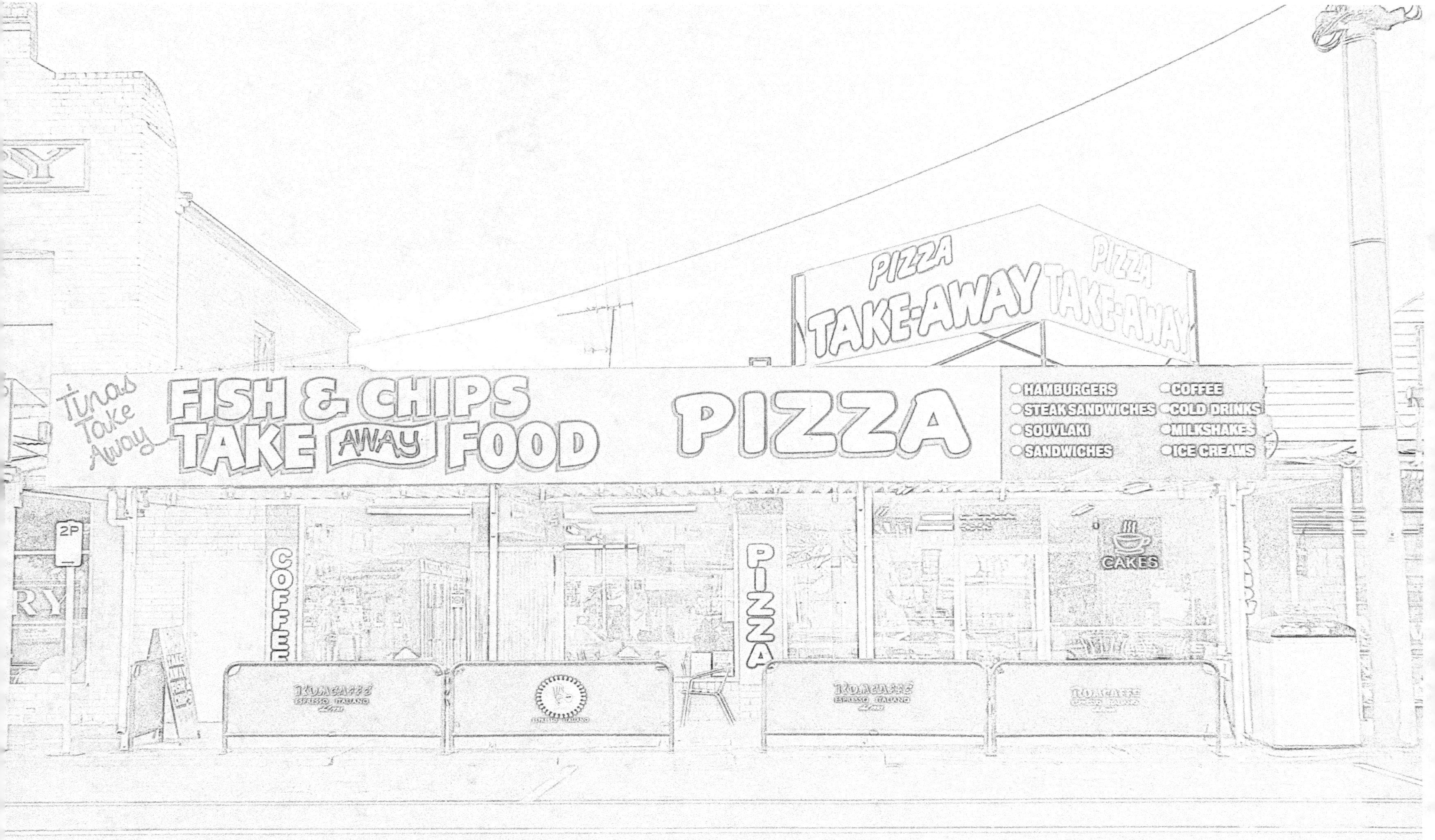
PIZZA
TAKE-AWAY
PIZZA
TAKE-AWAY
Tinas Take Away
FISH & CHIPS
TAKE AWAY FOOD
PIZZA
HAMBURGERS
STEAK SANDWICHES
SOUVLAKI
SANDWICHES
COFFEE
COLD DRINKS
MILKSHAKES
ICE CREAMS
2P
COFFEE
PIZZA
CAKES

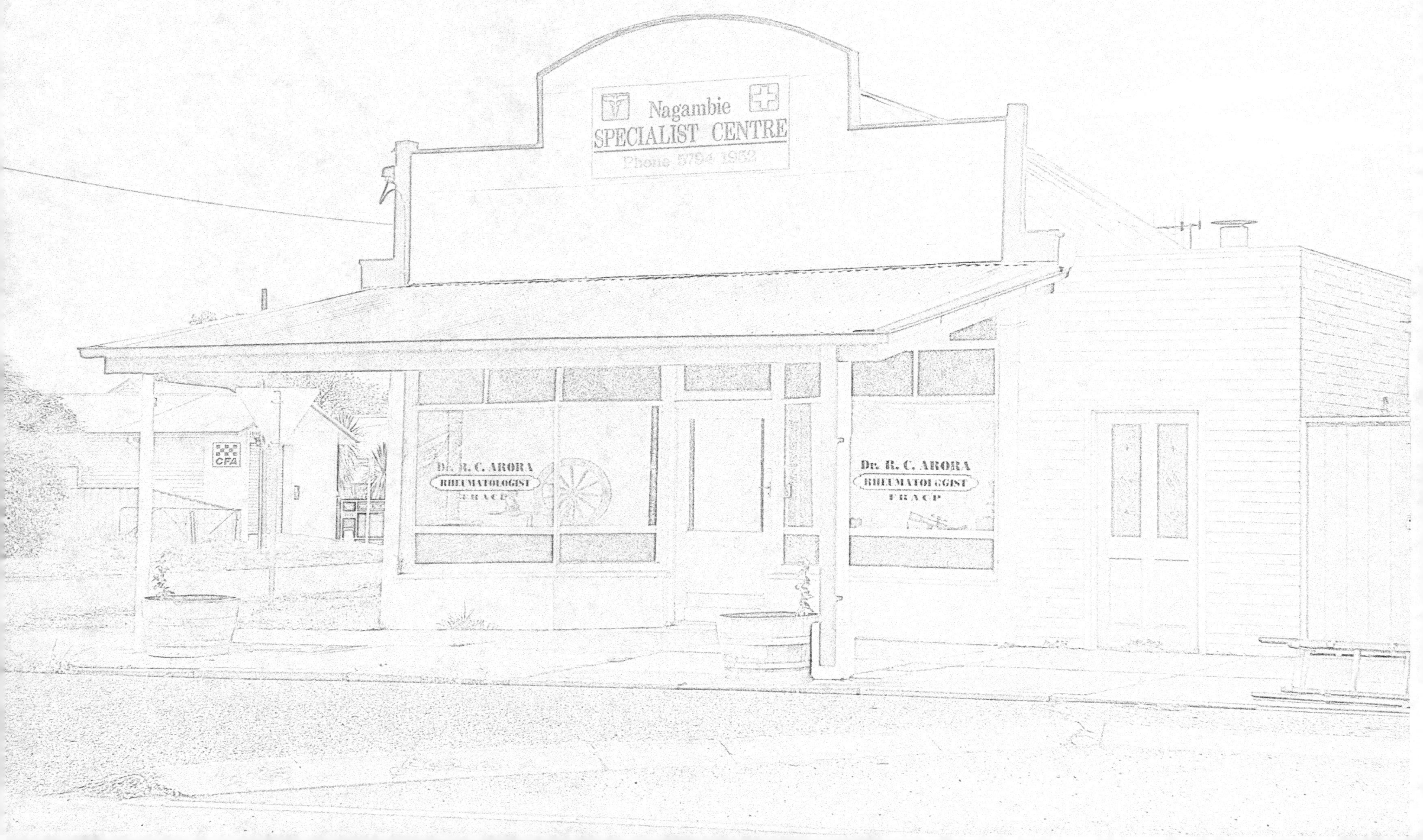
Nagambie
SPECIALIST CENTRE
Phone 5794 1952
CFA
Dr. R. C. ARORA
RHEUMATOLOGIST
FRACP

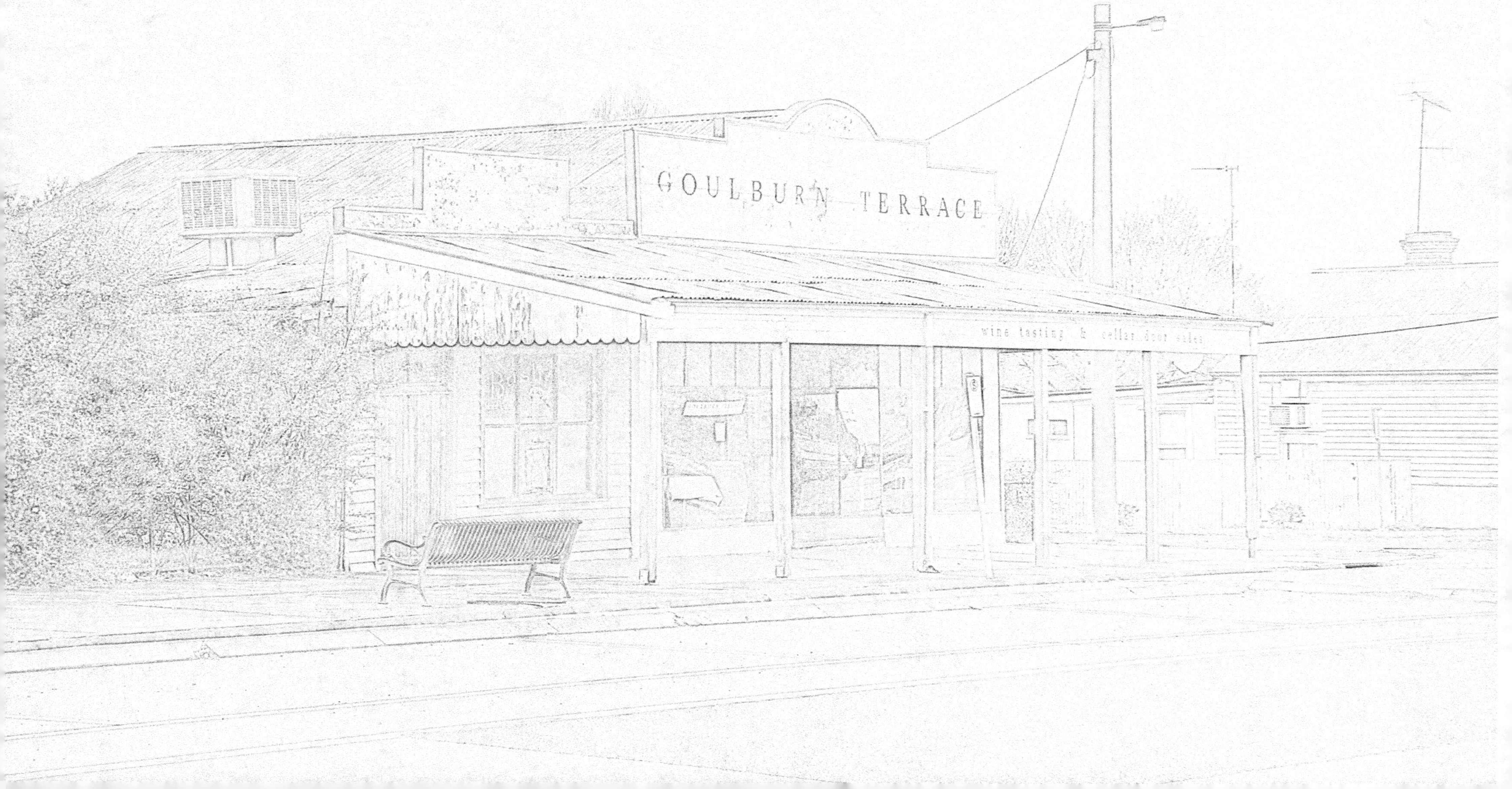
GOULBURN TERRACE
wine tasting & cellar door sales

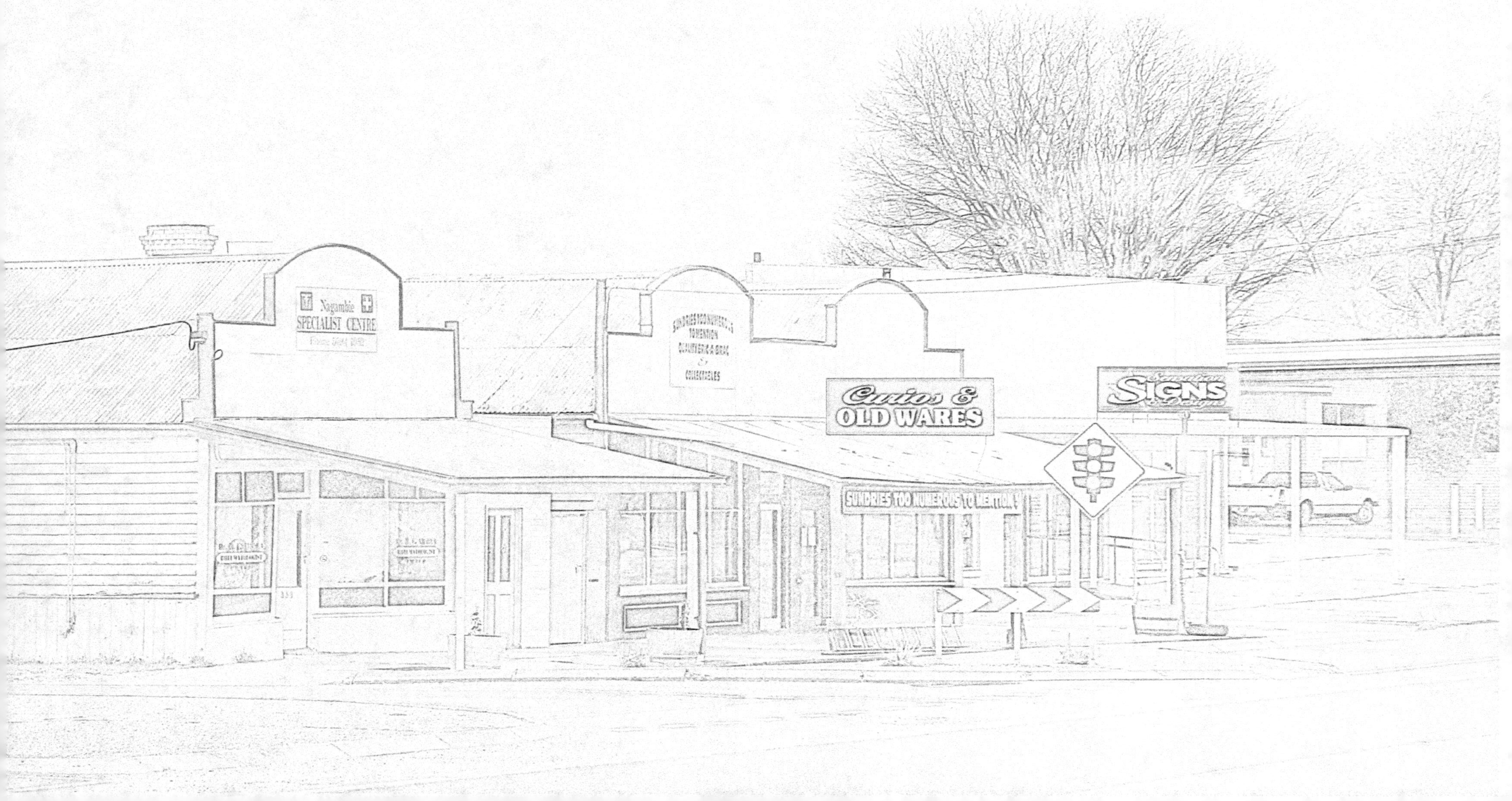
Nagambie
SPECIALIST CENTRE
Curios &
OLD WARES
SUNDRIES TOO NUMEROUS TO MENTION
SIGNS

VB
VICTORIA BITTER
DUNCAN'S DRIVE IN
TAB
SKY
BISTRO
HOTEL

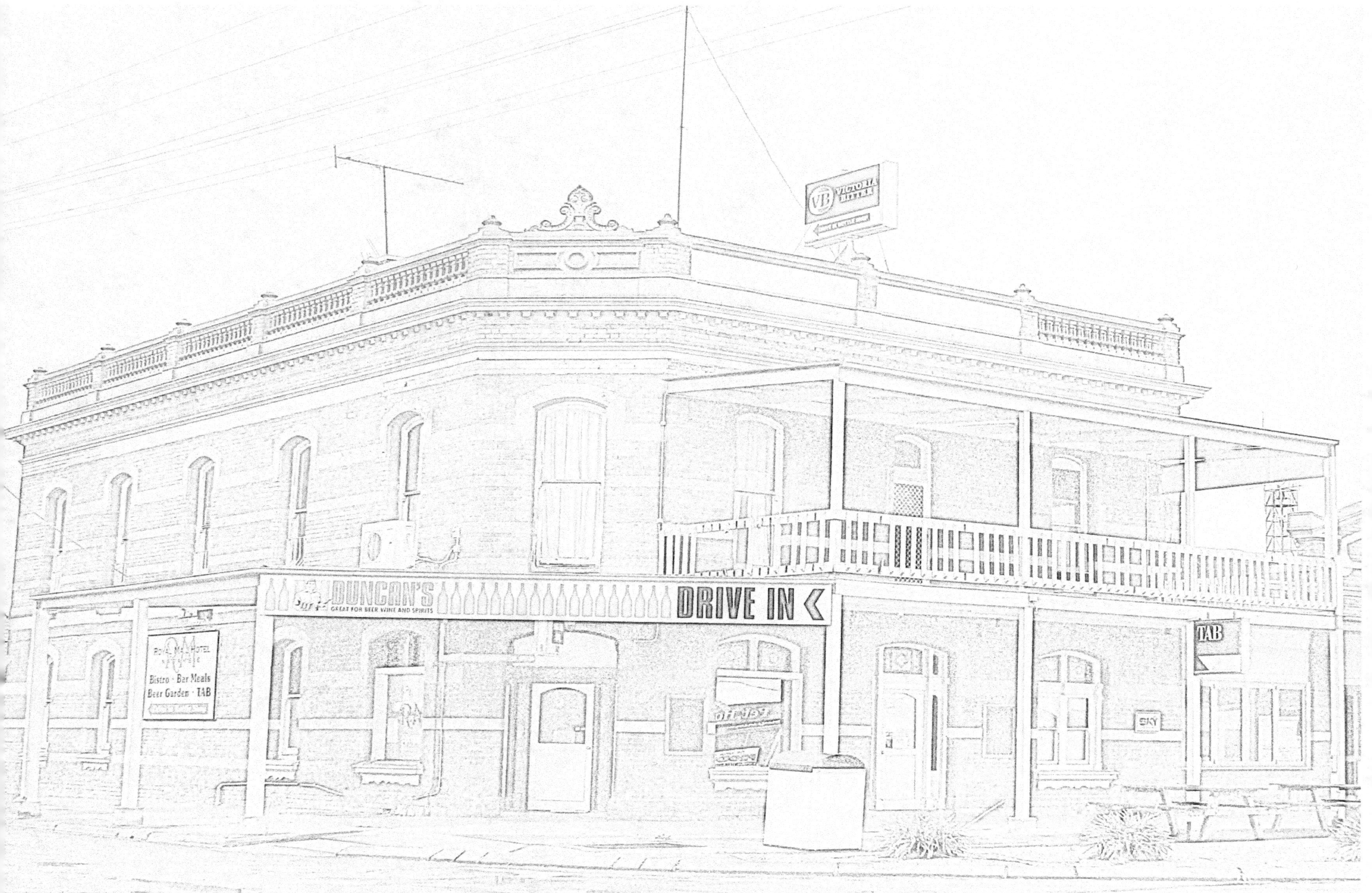
VB VICTORIA BITTER
DUNCAN'S
GREAT FOR BEER WINE AND SPIRITS
DRIVE IN
Bistro · Bar Meals
Beer Garden · TAB
TAB
SKY

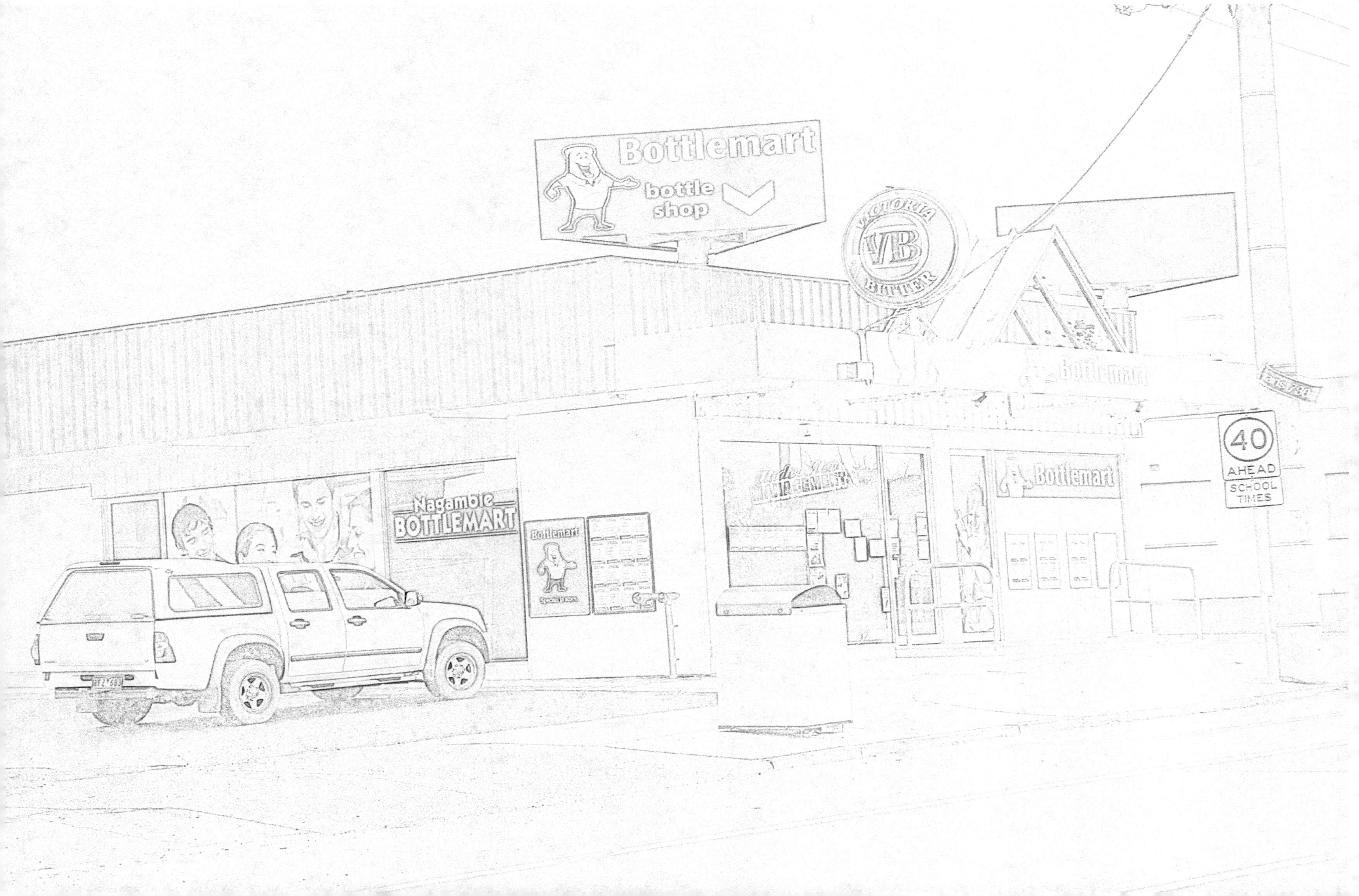
Bottlemart
bottle
shop
VICTORIA
VB
BITTER
Bottlemart
Nagambie
BOTTLEMART
Bottlemart
Bottlemart
40
AHEAD
SCHOOL
TIMES

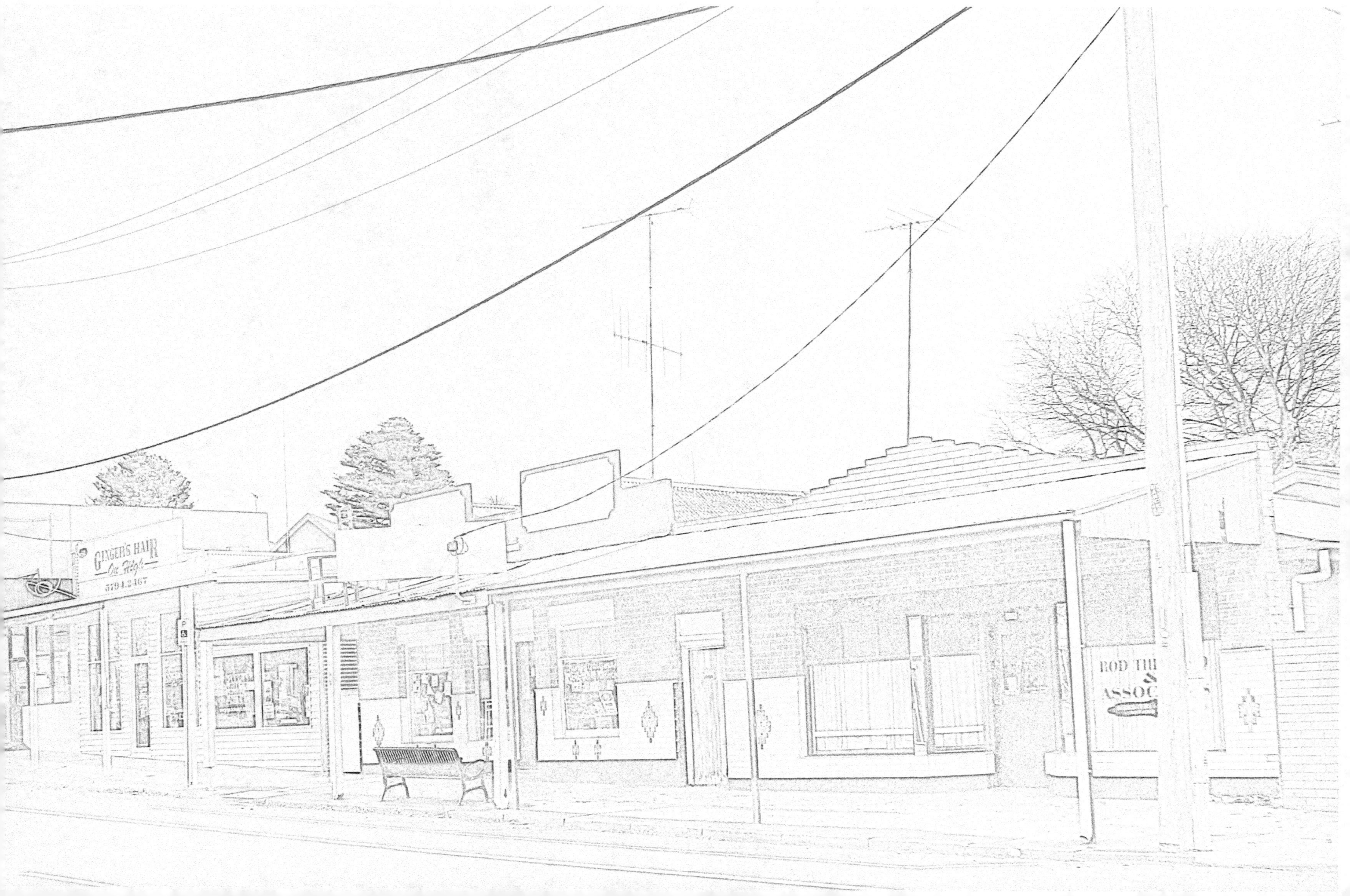
GINGER'S HAIR
On High

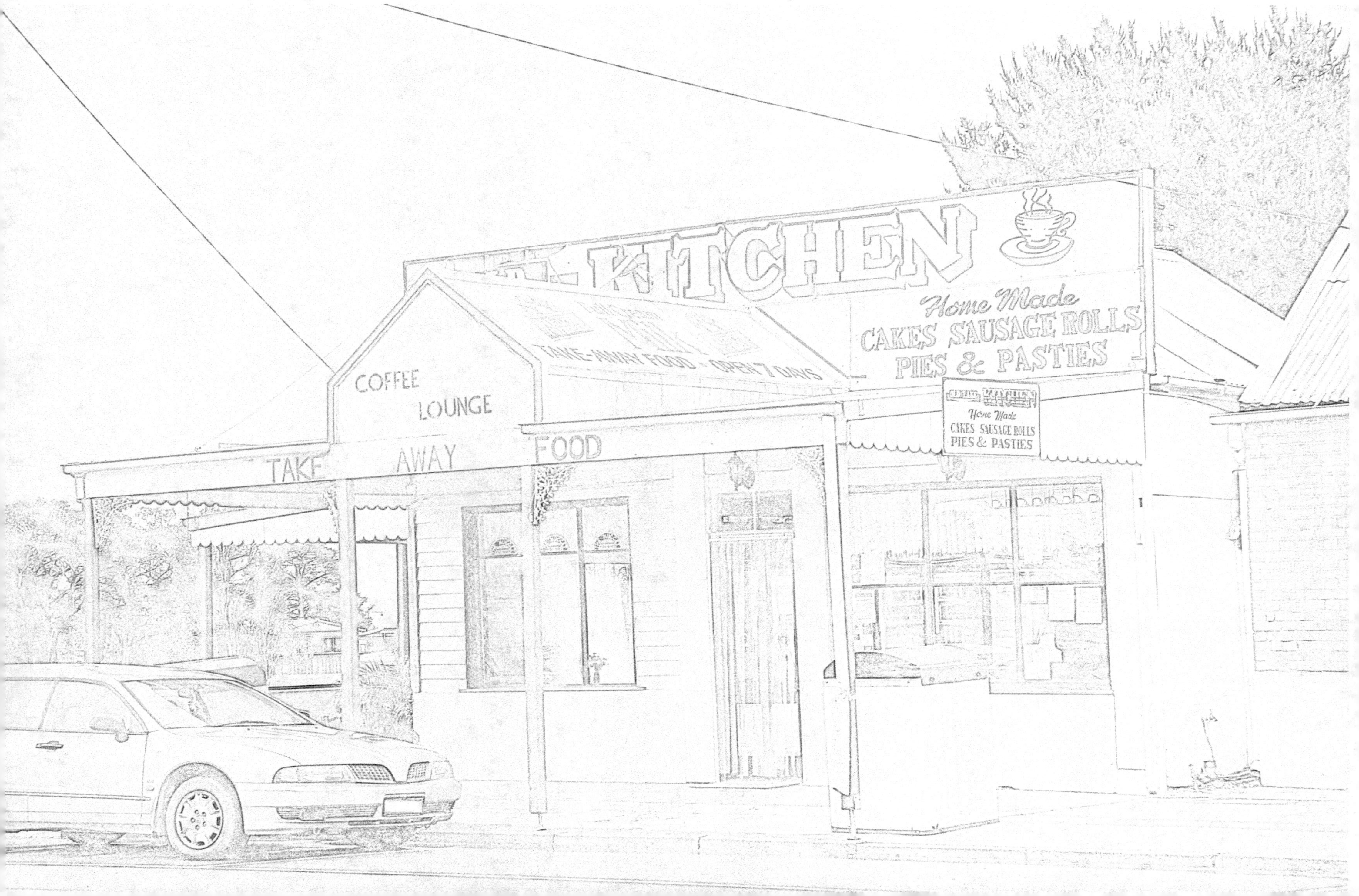
KITCHEN
Home Made
CAKES SAUSAGE ROLLS
PIES & PASTIES
TAKE-AWAY FOOD - OPEN 7 DAYS
COFFEE
LOUNGE
TAKE
AWAY
FOOD
Home Made
CAKES SAUSAGE ROLLS
PIES & PASTIES

COURTHOUSE INN
BED & BREAKFAST
ANTIQUES
Police
40

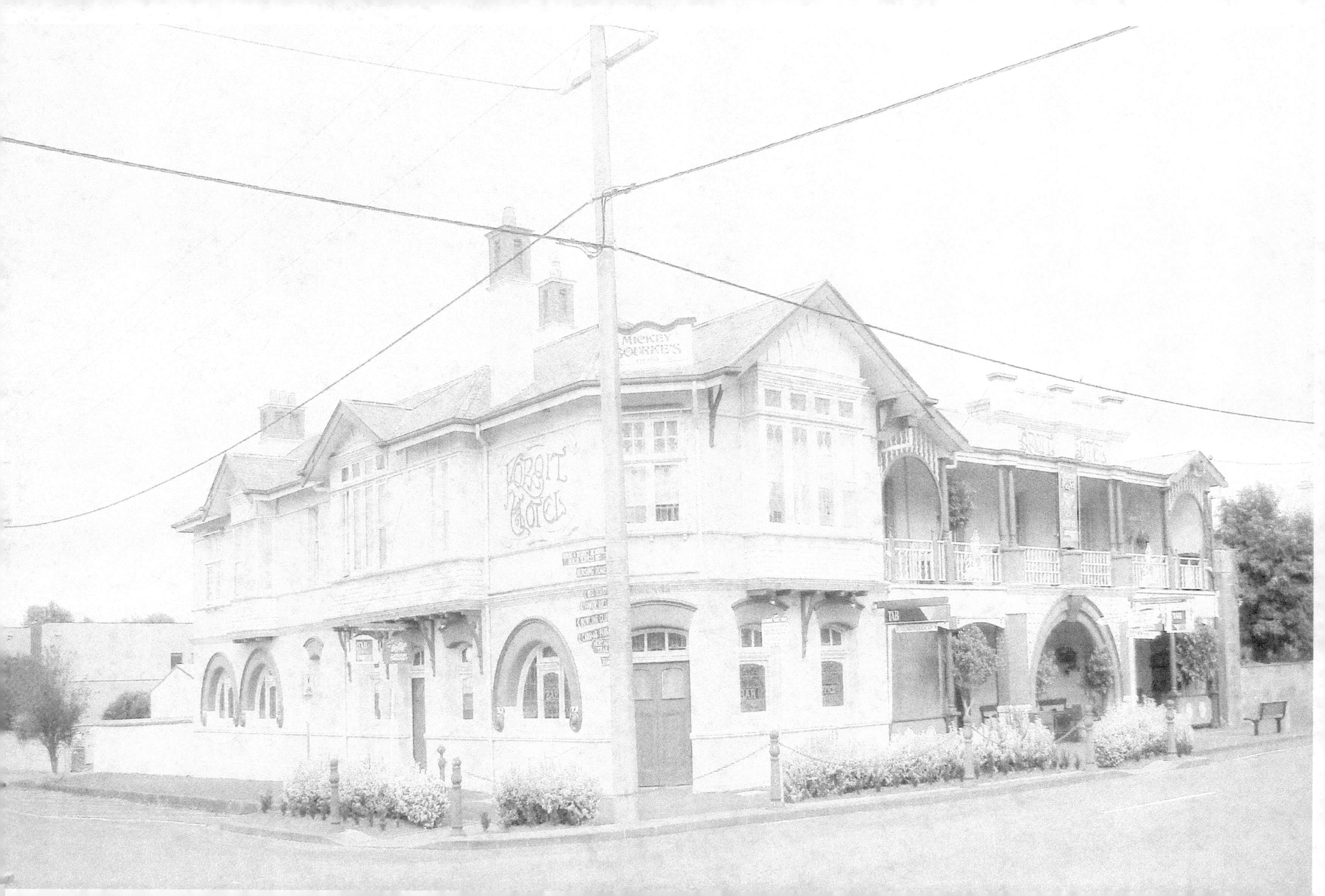
MICKEY BOURKE'S
TAB

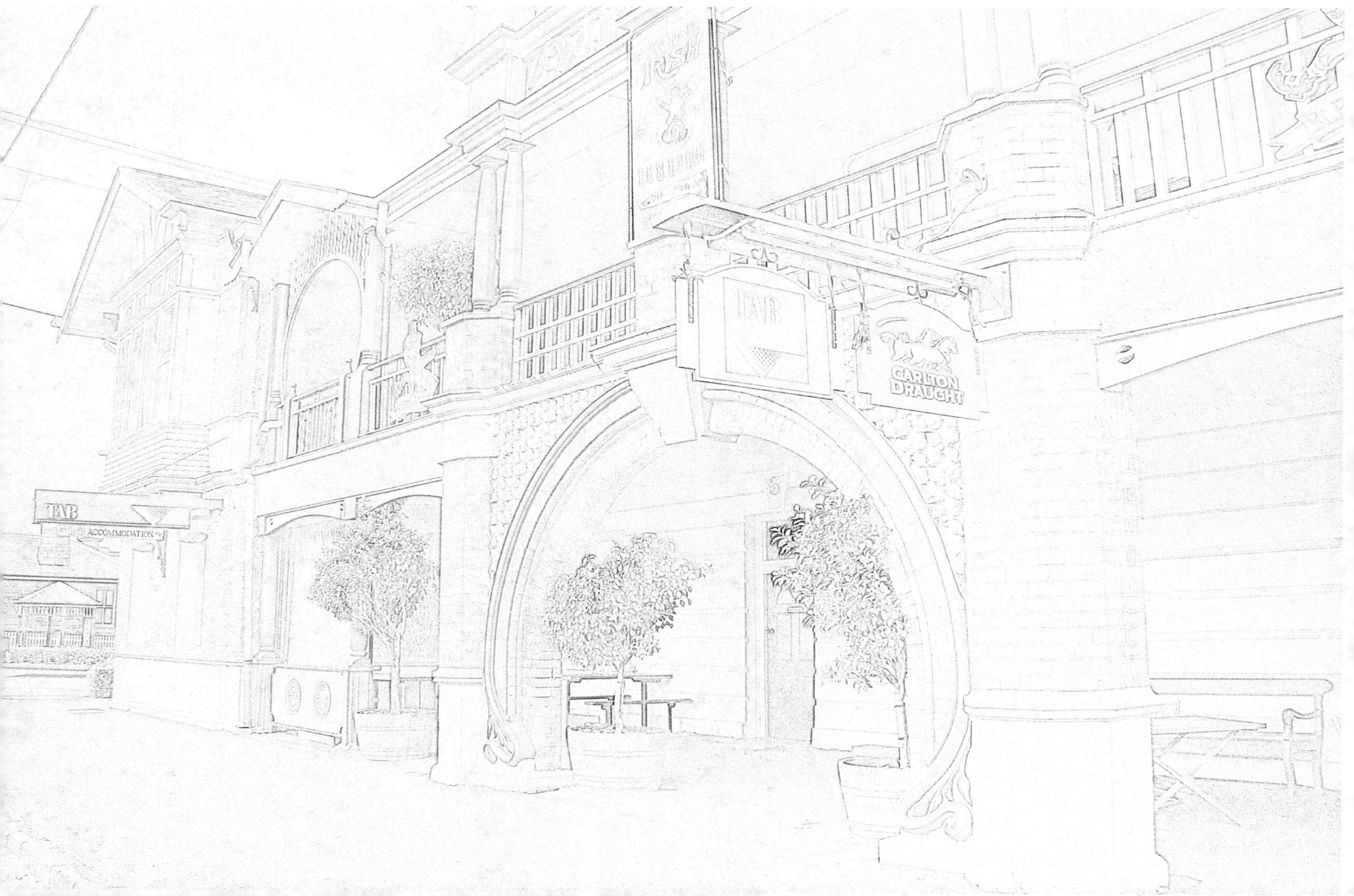
TAB
CARLTON
DRAUGHT
TAB
ACCOMMODATION

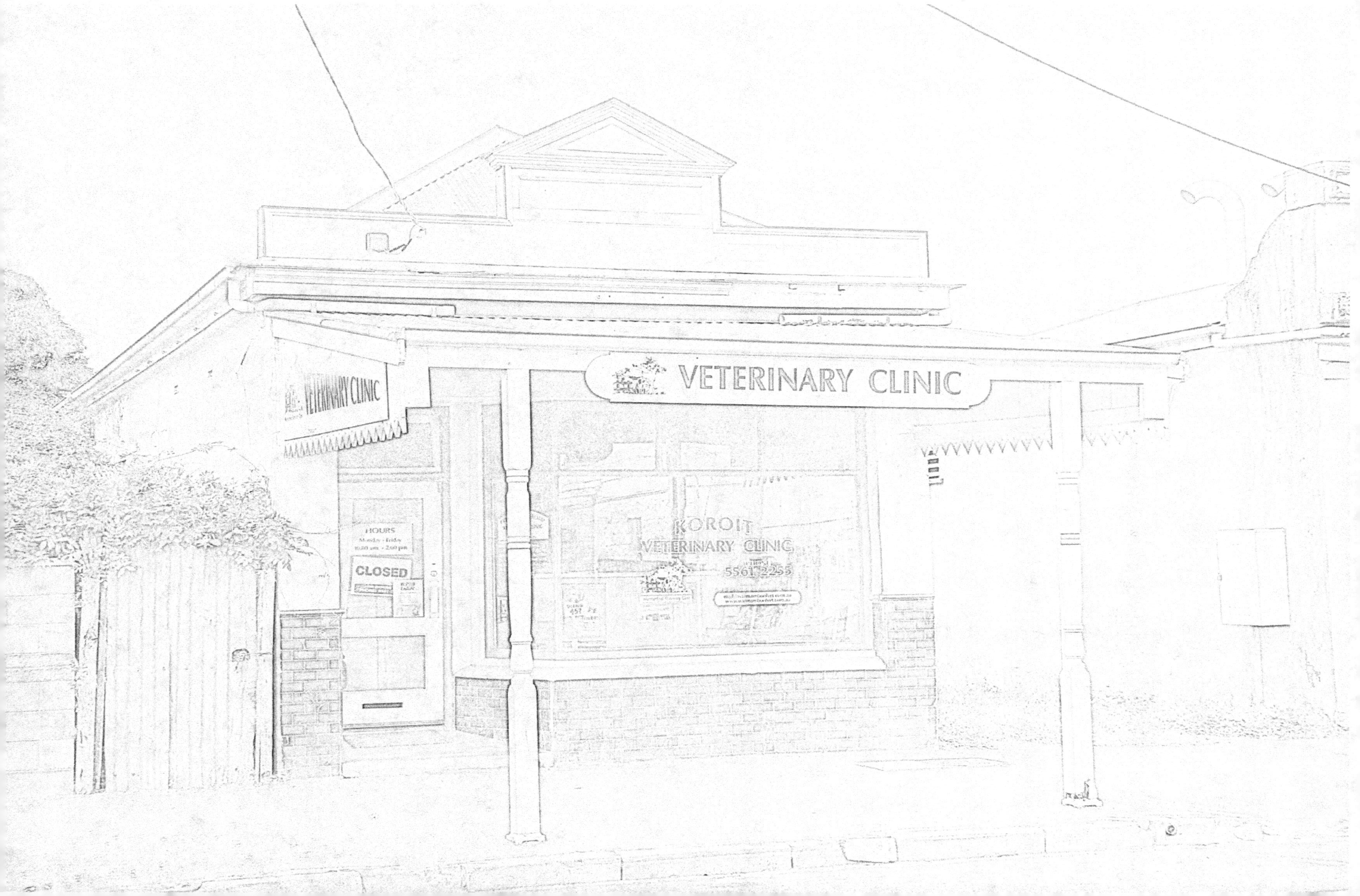
VETERINARY CLINIC
VETERINARY CLINIC
HOURS
CLOSED
KOROIT
VETERINARY CLINIC
5561 2255

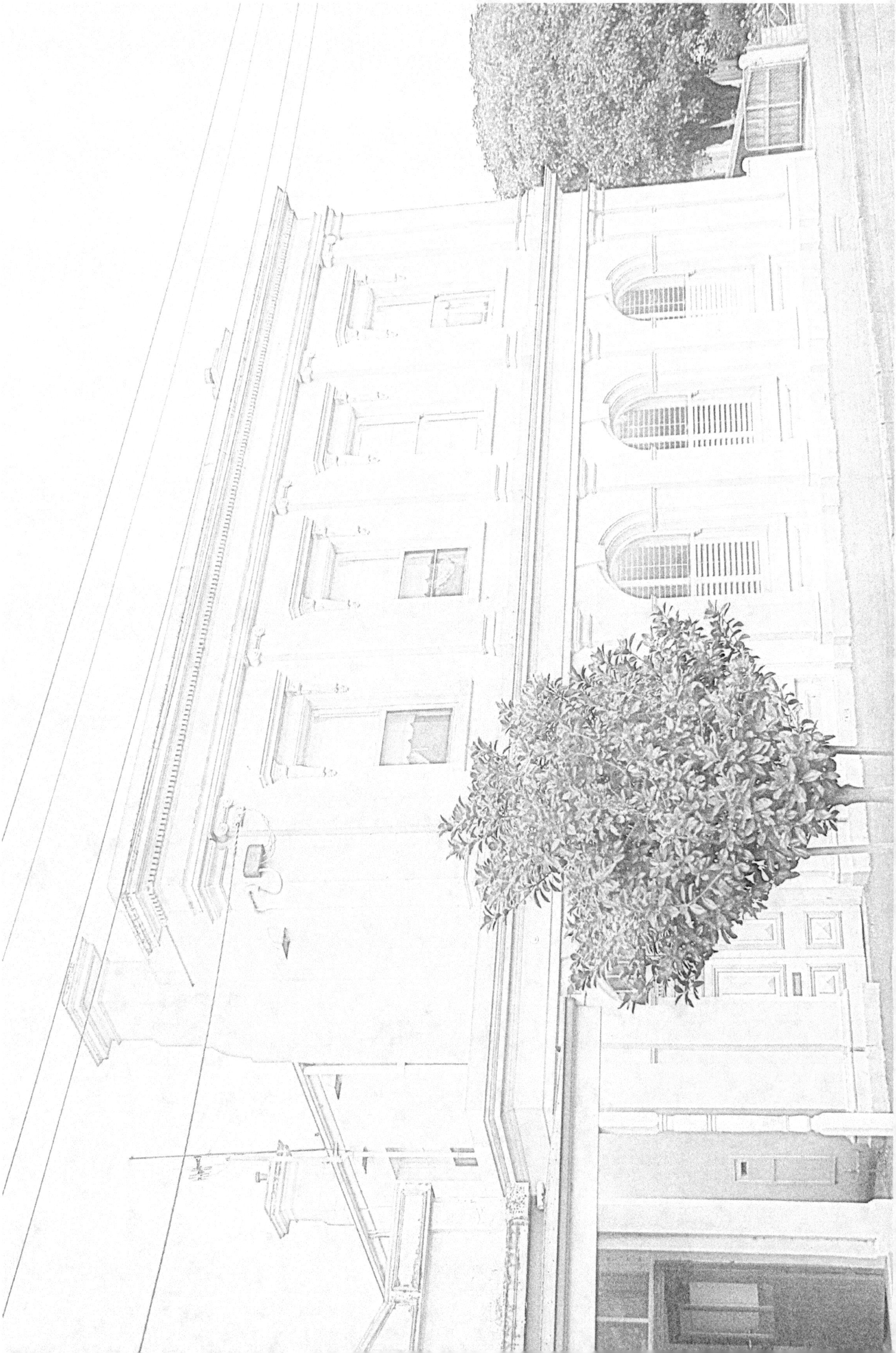

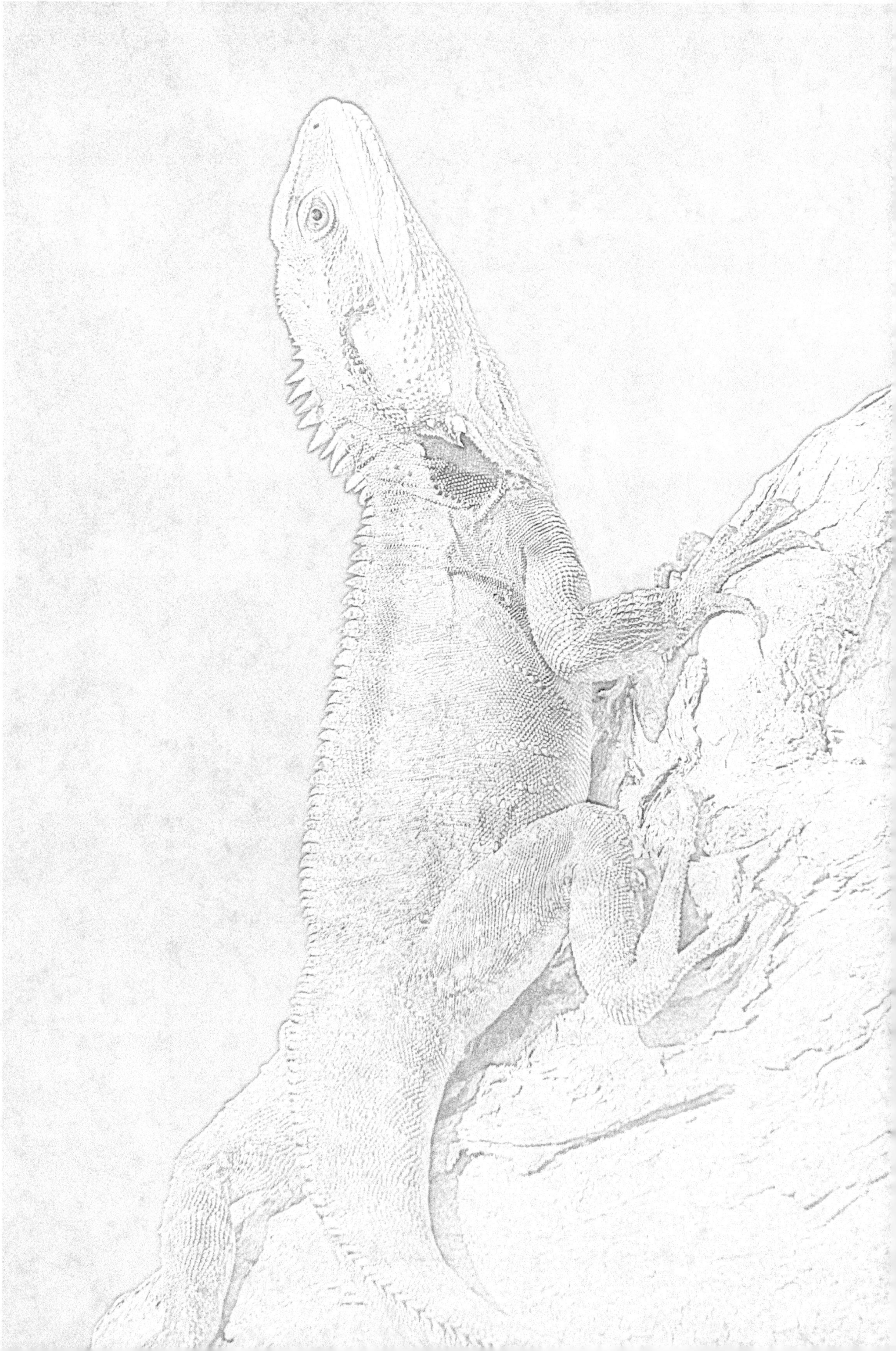

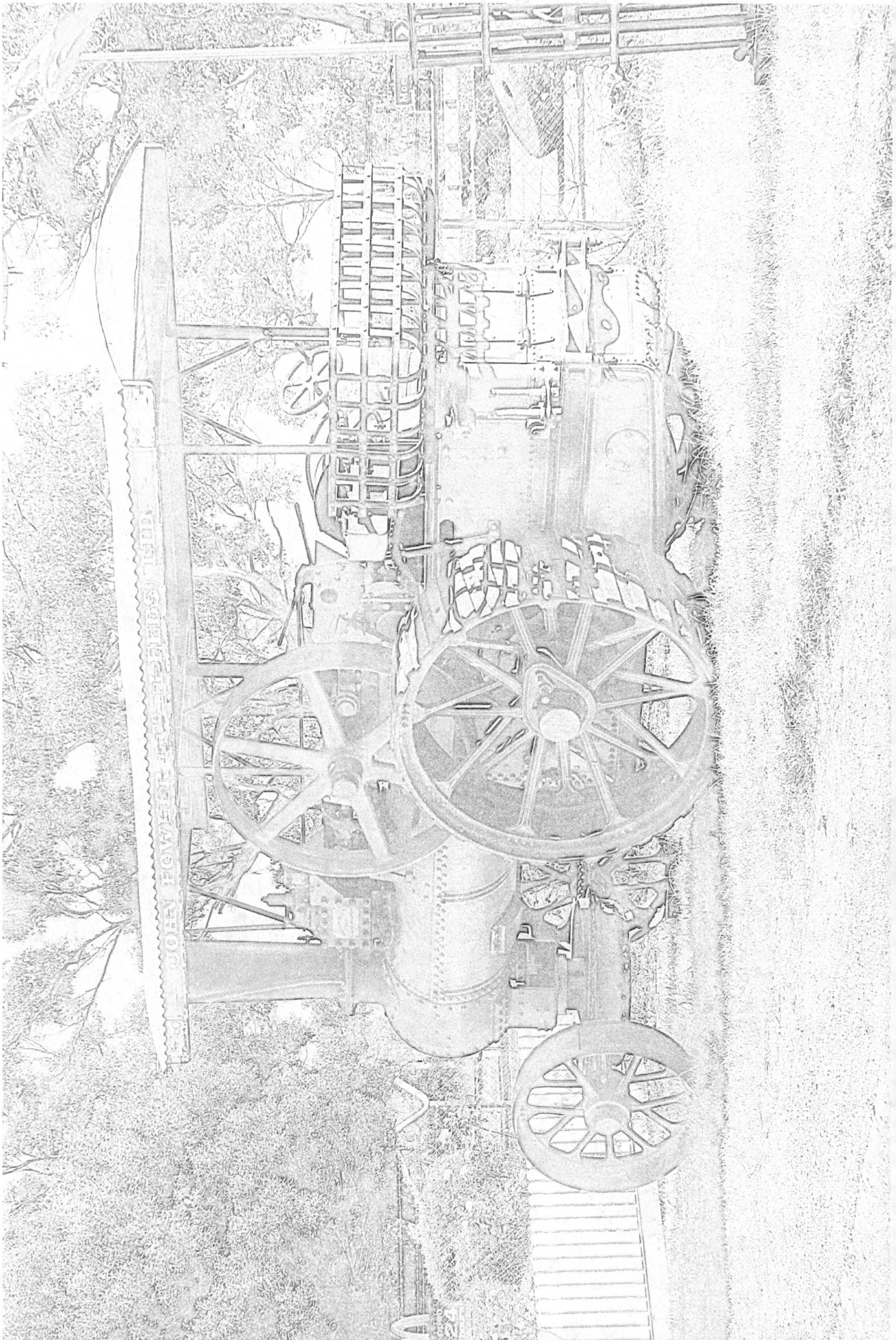
JOHN FOWLER
(LEEDS) LTD

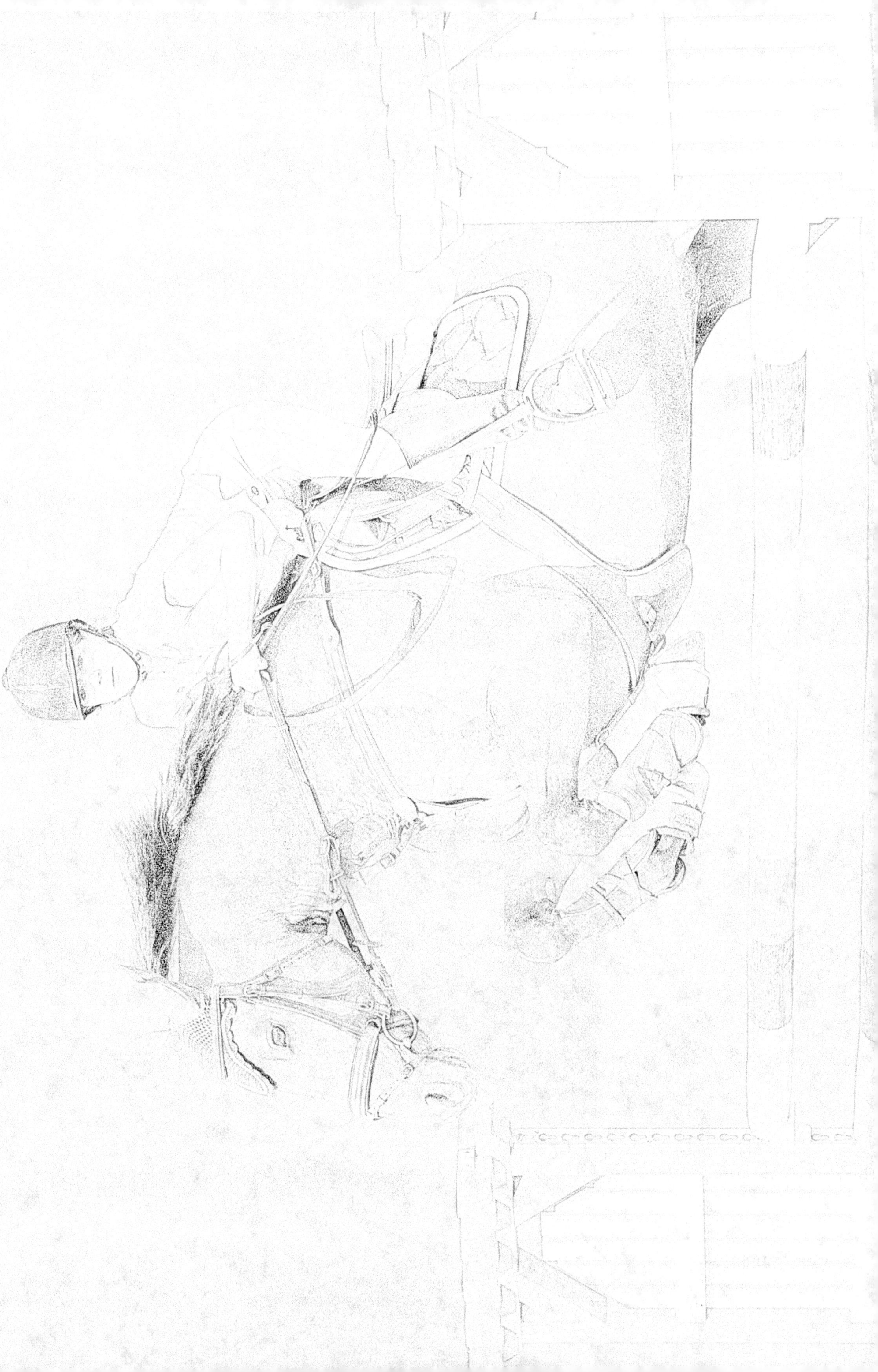

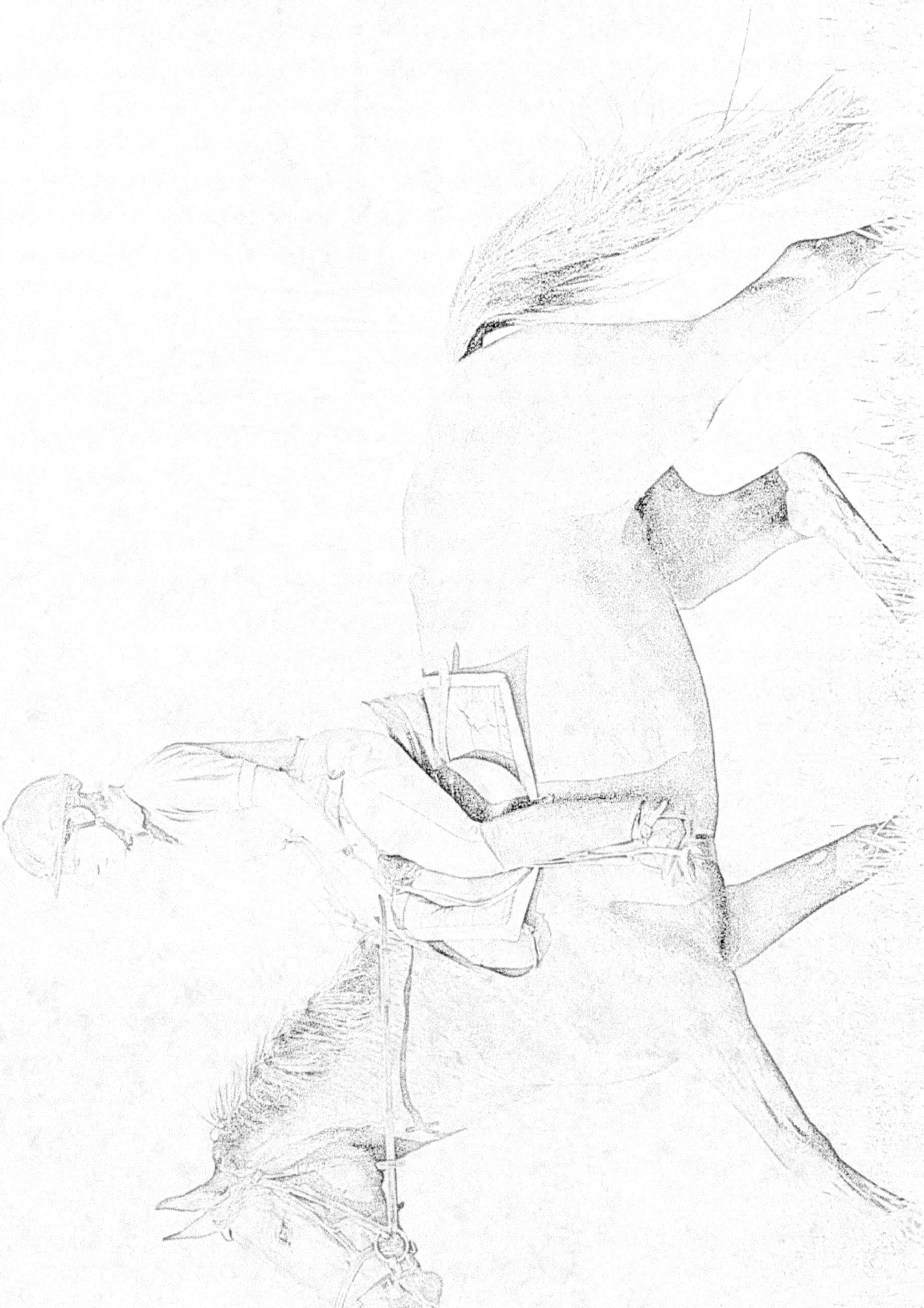

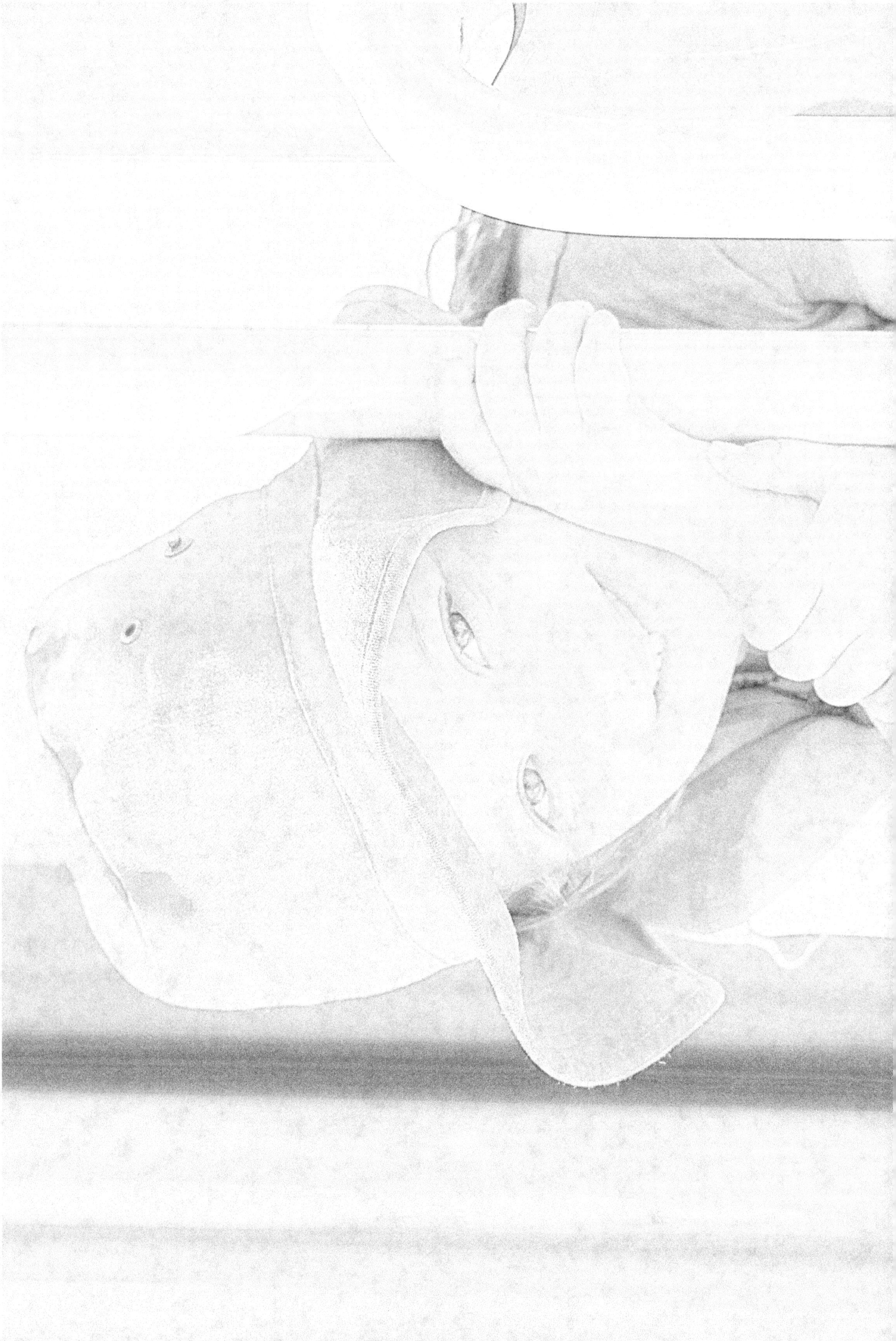

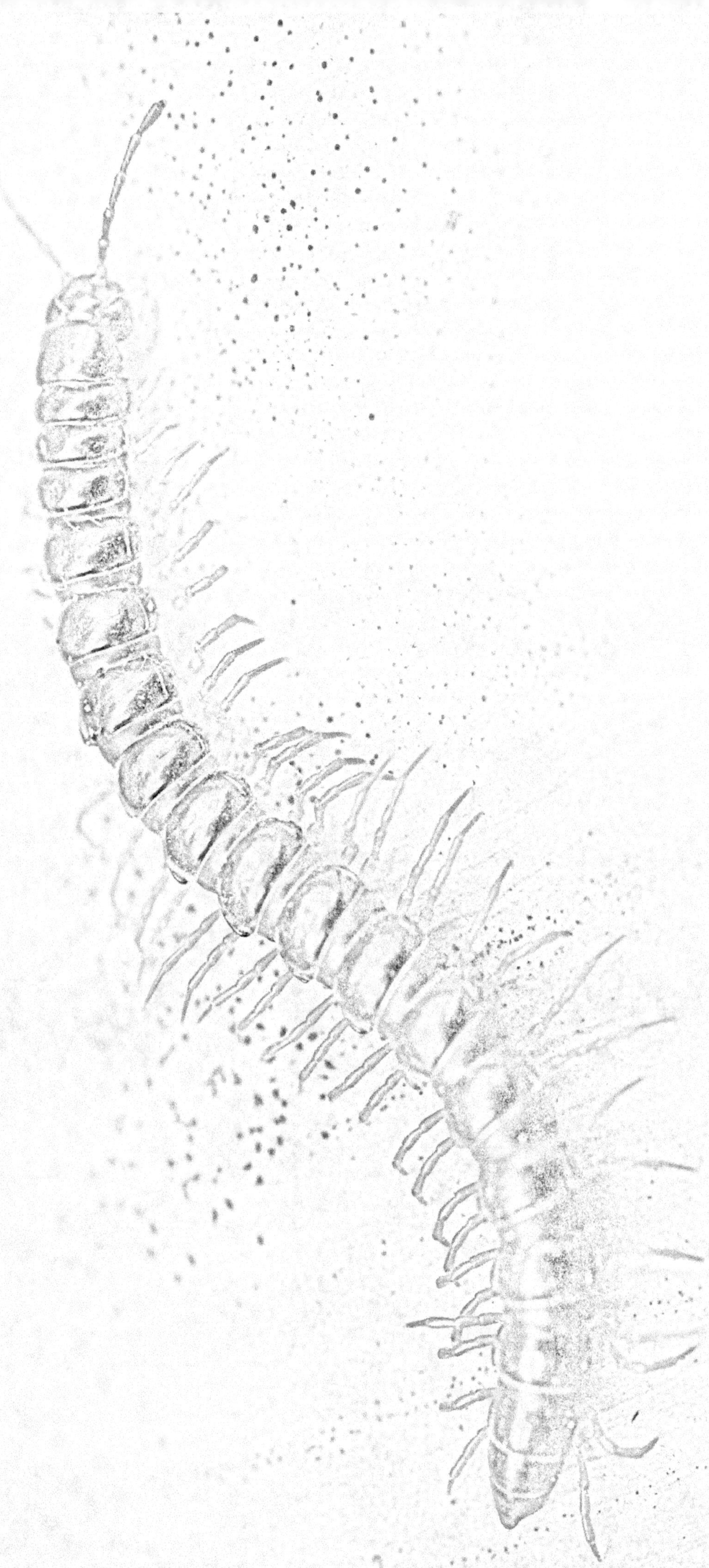

ESTD 1888
CHEMIST
AND
DRUGGIST
Bogan LollyShop & Gifts
Bogan LollyShop
Gifts
A SUGAR RUSH IN THE OUTBACK!
for
HAIR
LADIES & MENS
SALON
GIFTS
FINE CH

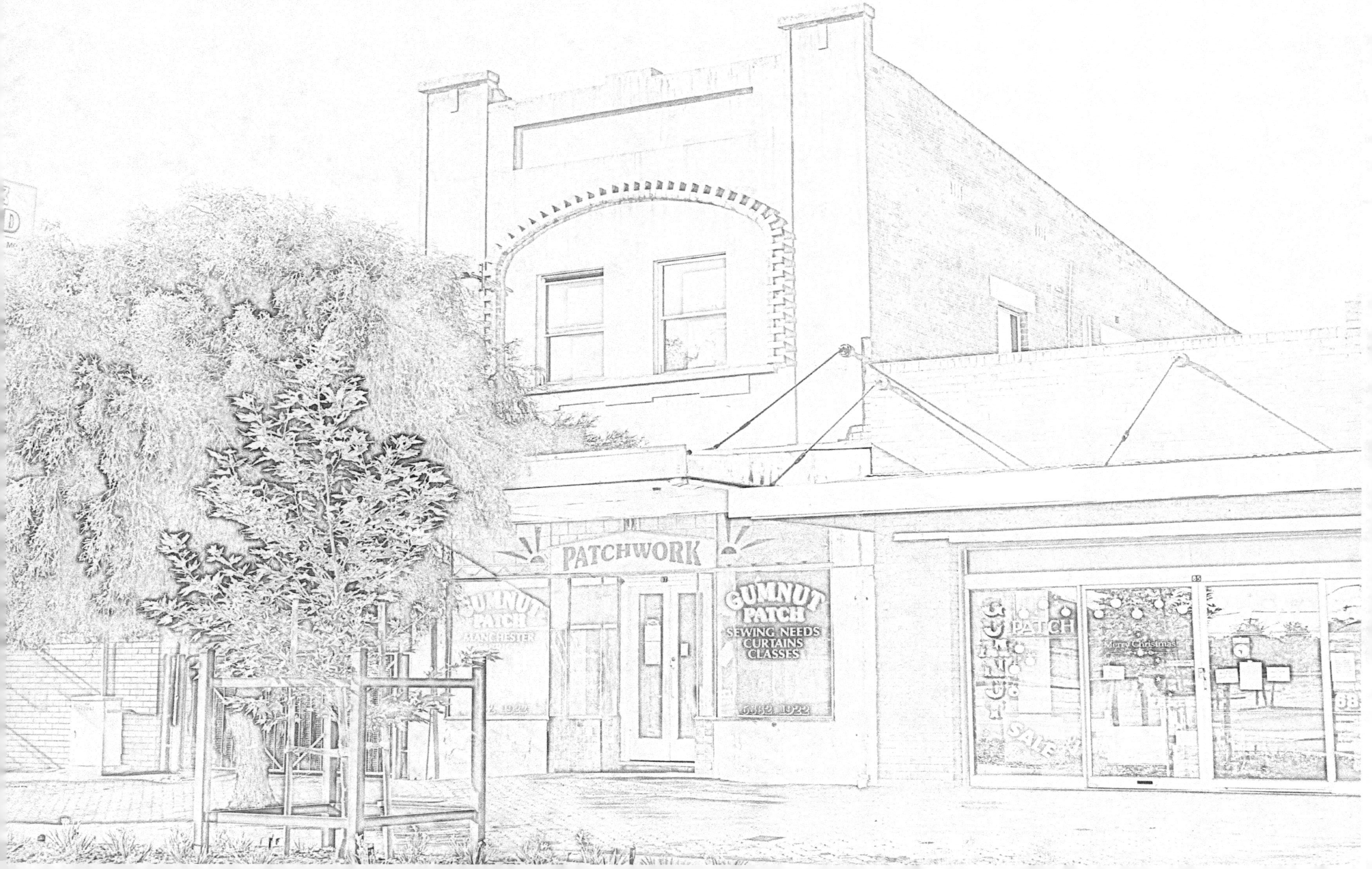
PATCHWORK
GUMNUT PATCH
SEWING NEEDS
CURTAINS
CLASSES
6332 1922
GUMNUT PATCH
MANCHESTER
PATCH
Merry Christmas!
SALE

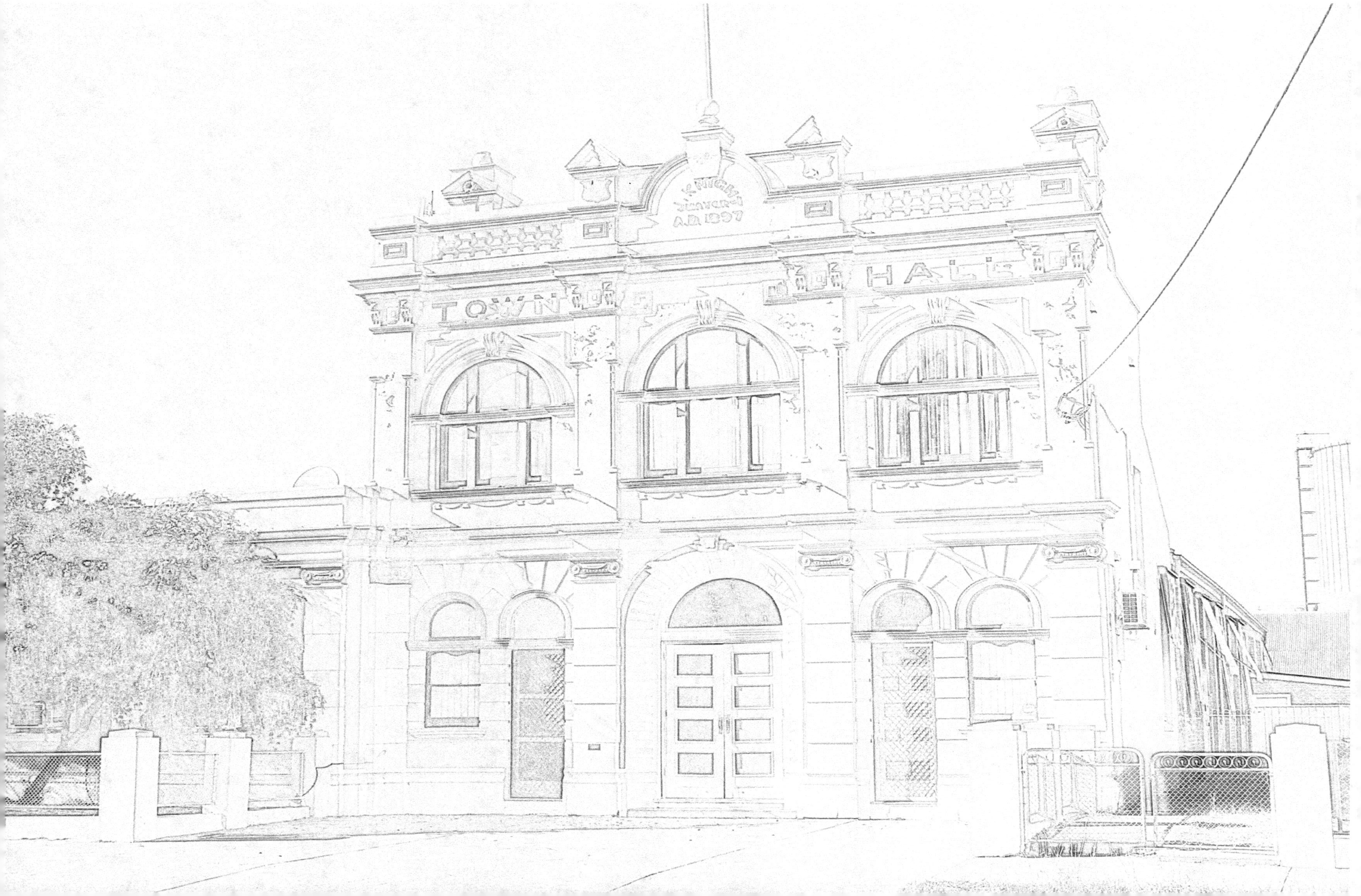
TOWN
HALL

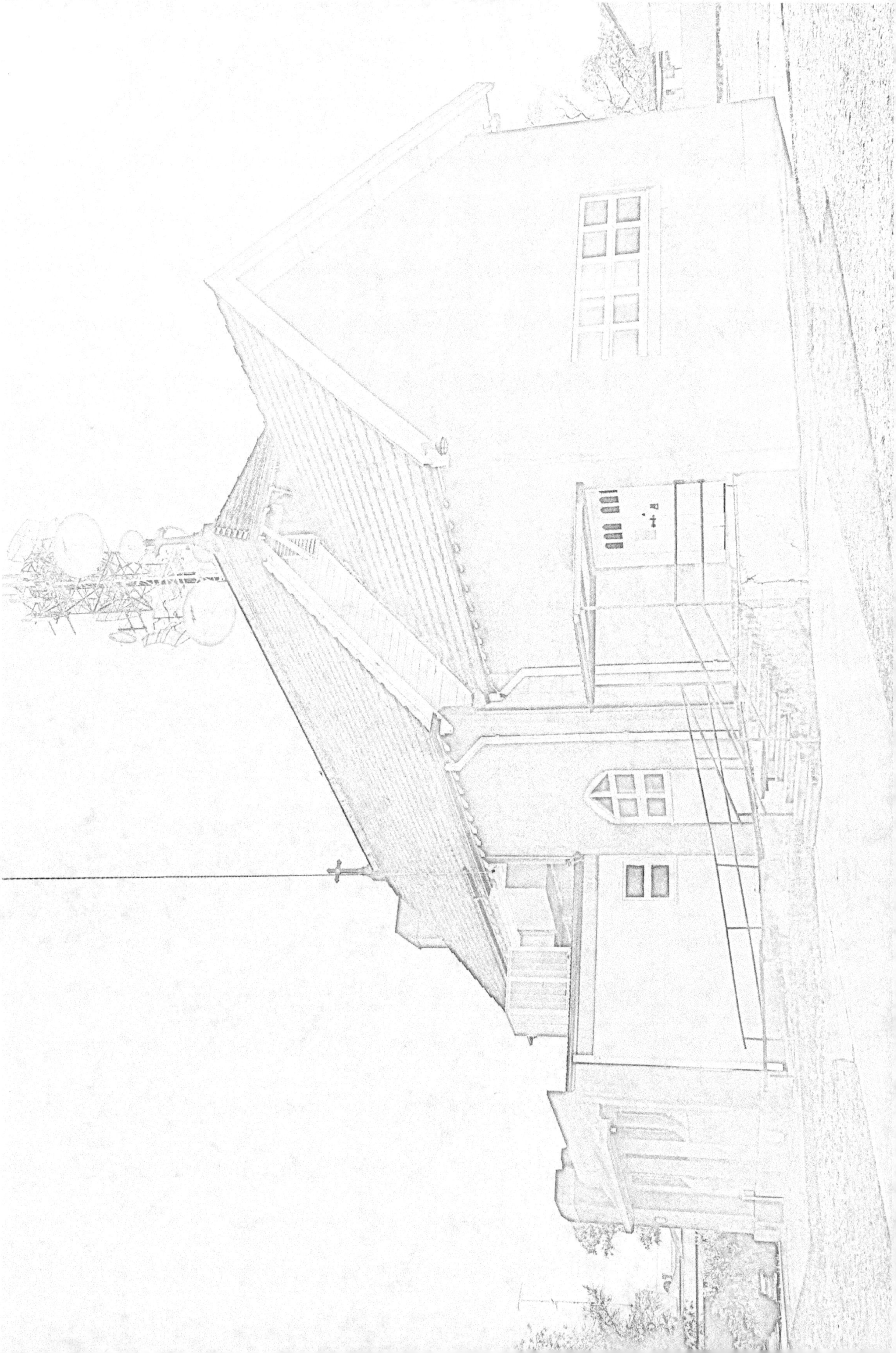

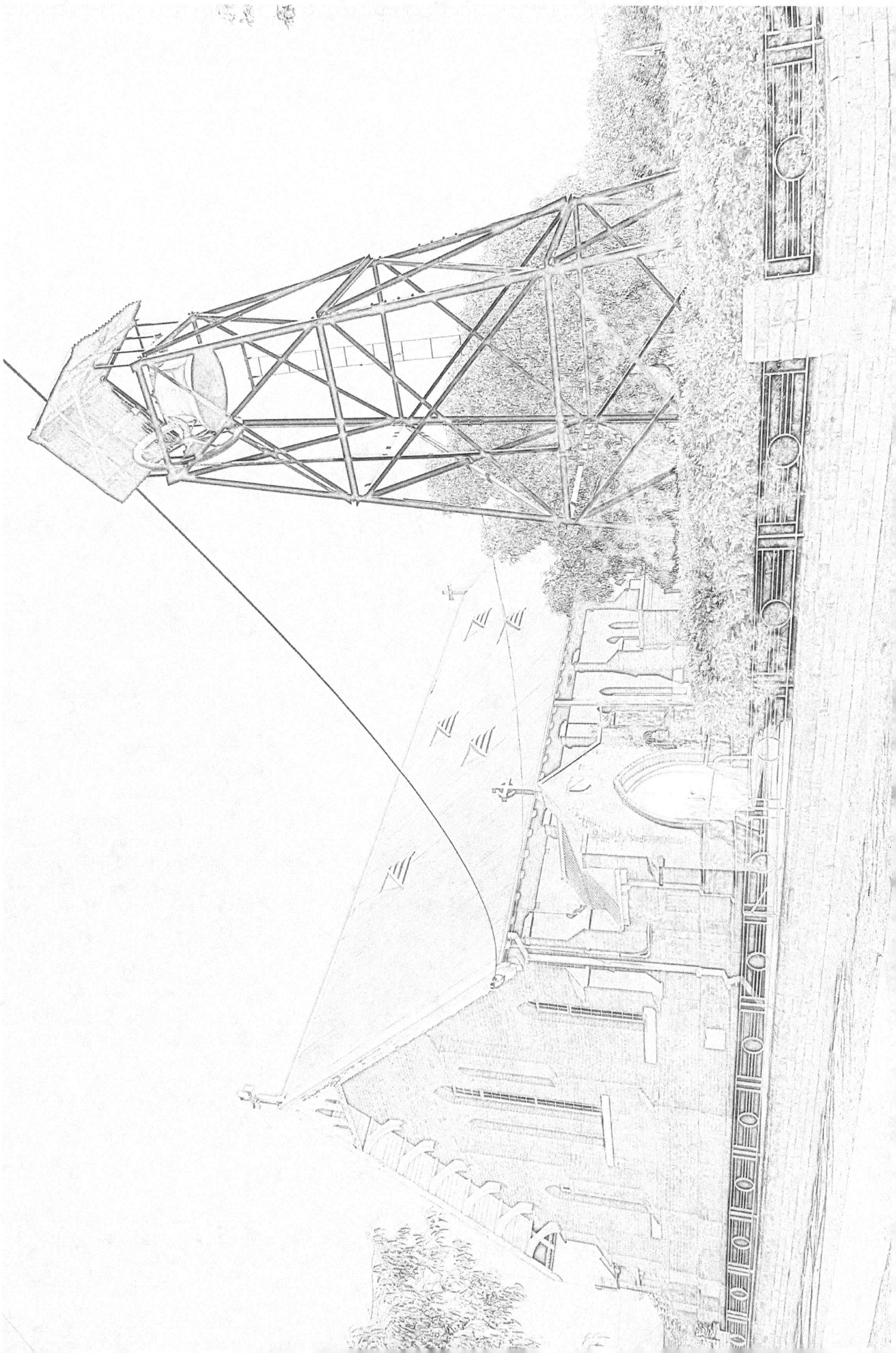

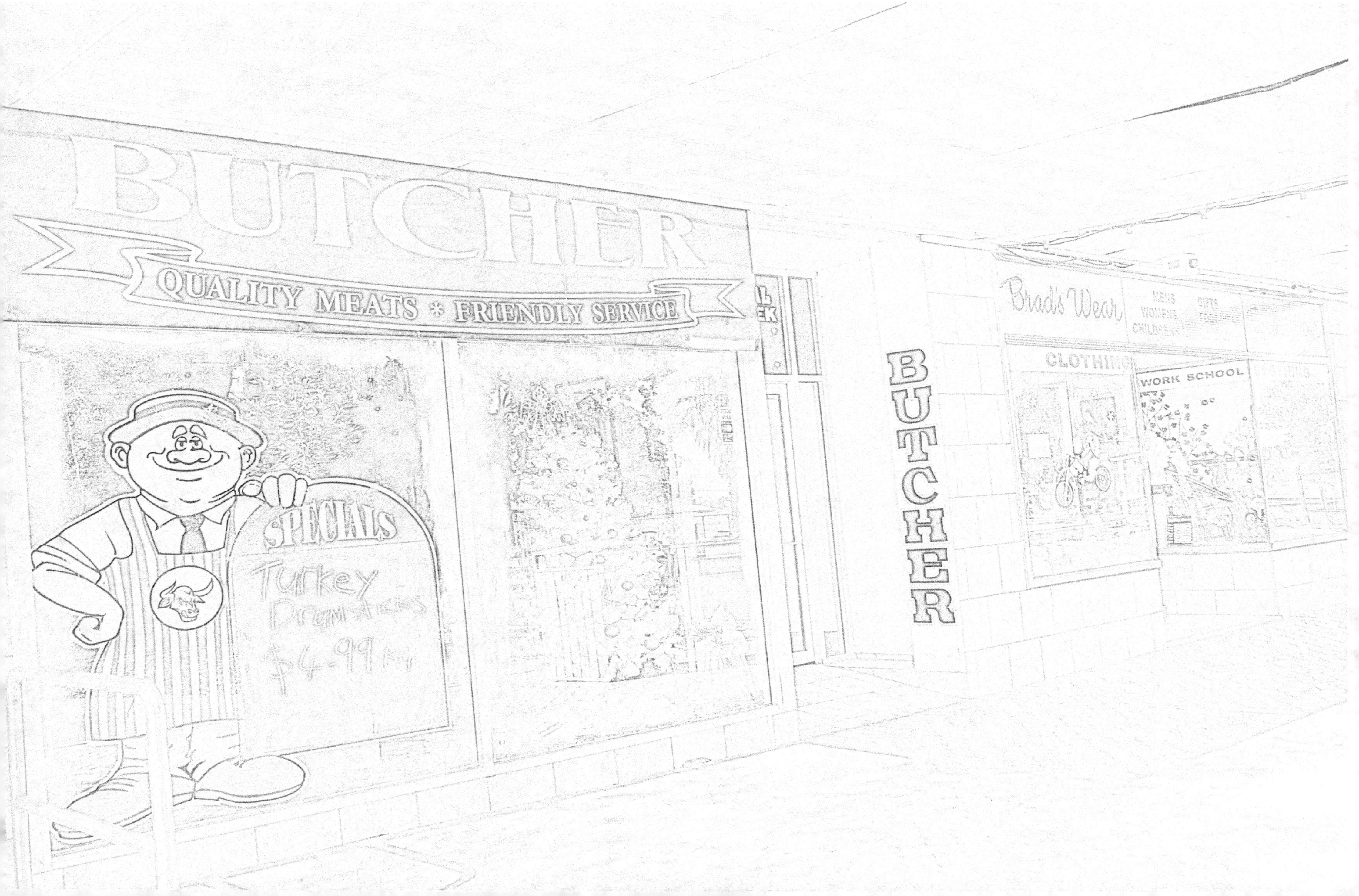
BUTCHER
QUALITY MEATS * FRIENDLY SERVICE
SPECIALS
Turkey
Drumsticks
$4.99 kg
BUTCHER
Brad's Wear
MENS
WOMENS
CHILDRENS
GIFTS
CLOTHING
WORK SCHOOL

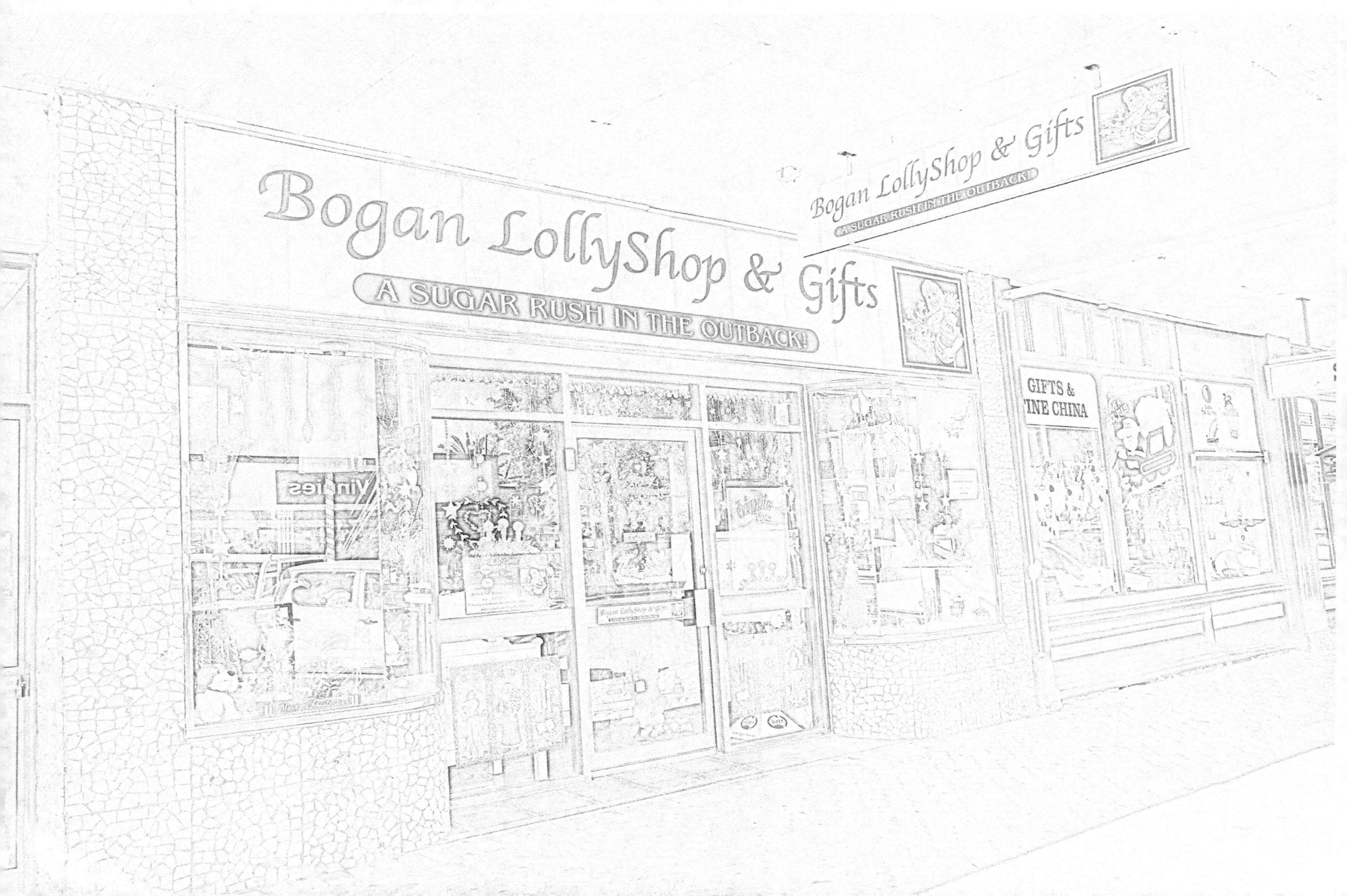
Bogan LollyShop & Gifts
A SUGAR RUSH IN THE OUTBACK!
Bogan LollyShop & Gifts
A SUGAR RUSH IN THE OUTBACK!
GIFTS &
FINE CHINA

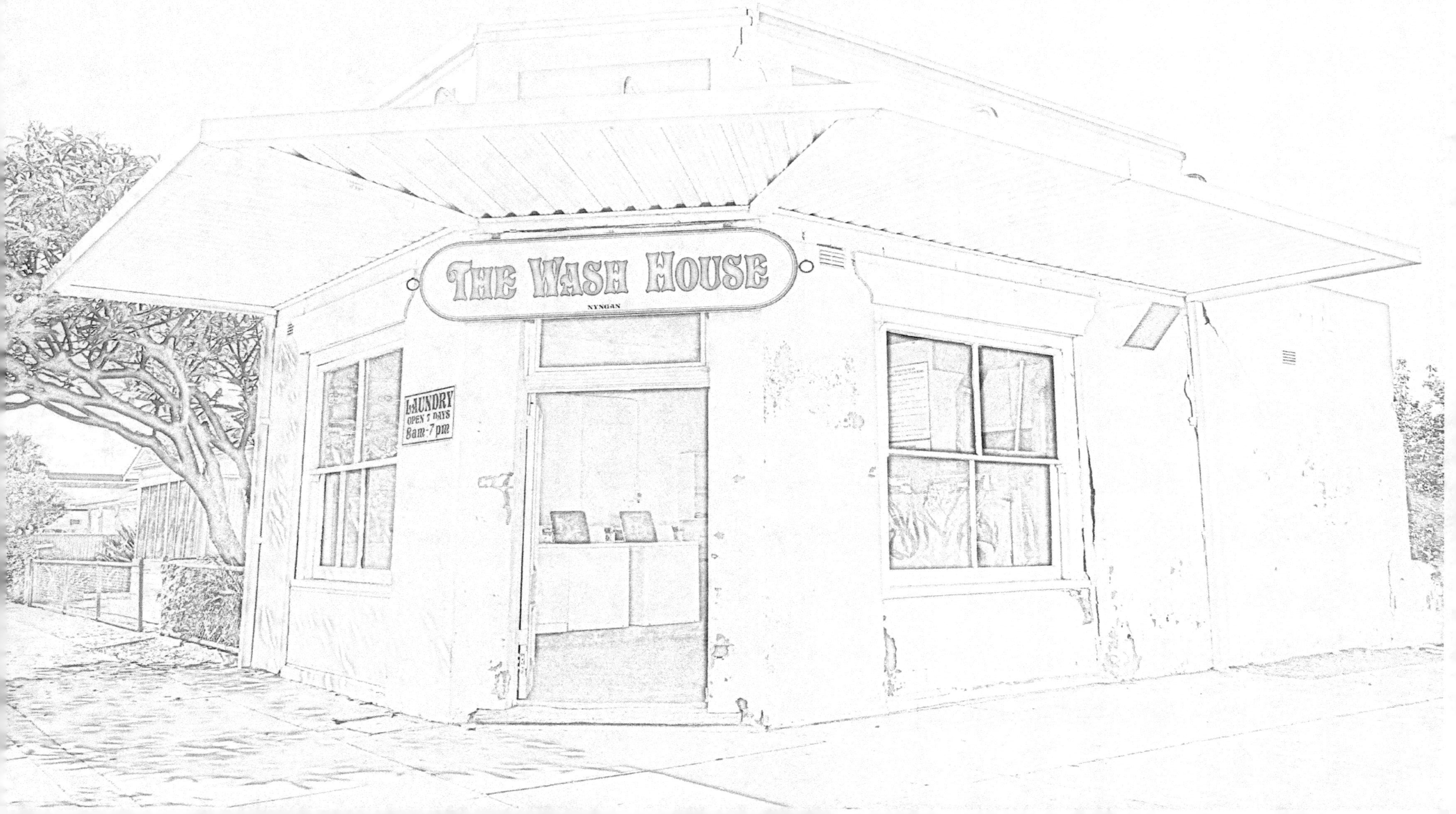
THE WASH HOUSE
NYNGAN
LAUNDRY
OPEN 7 DAYS
8am-7pm

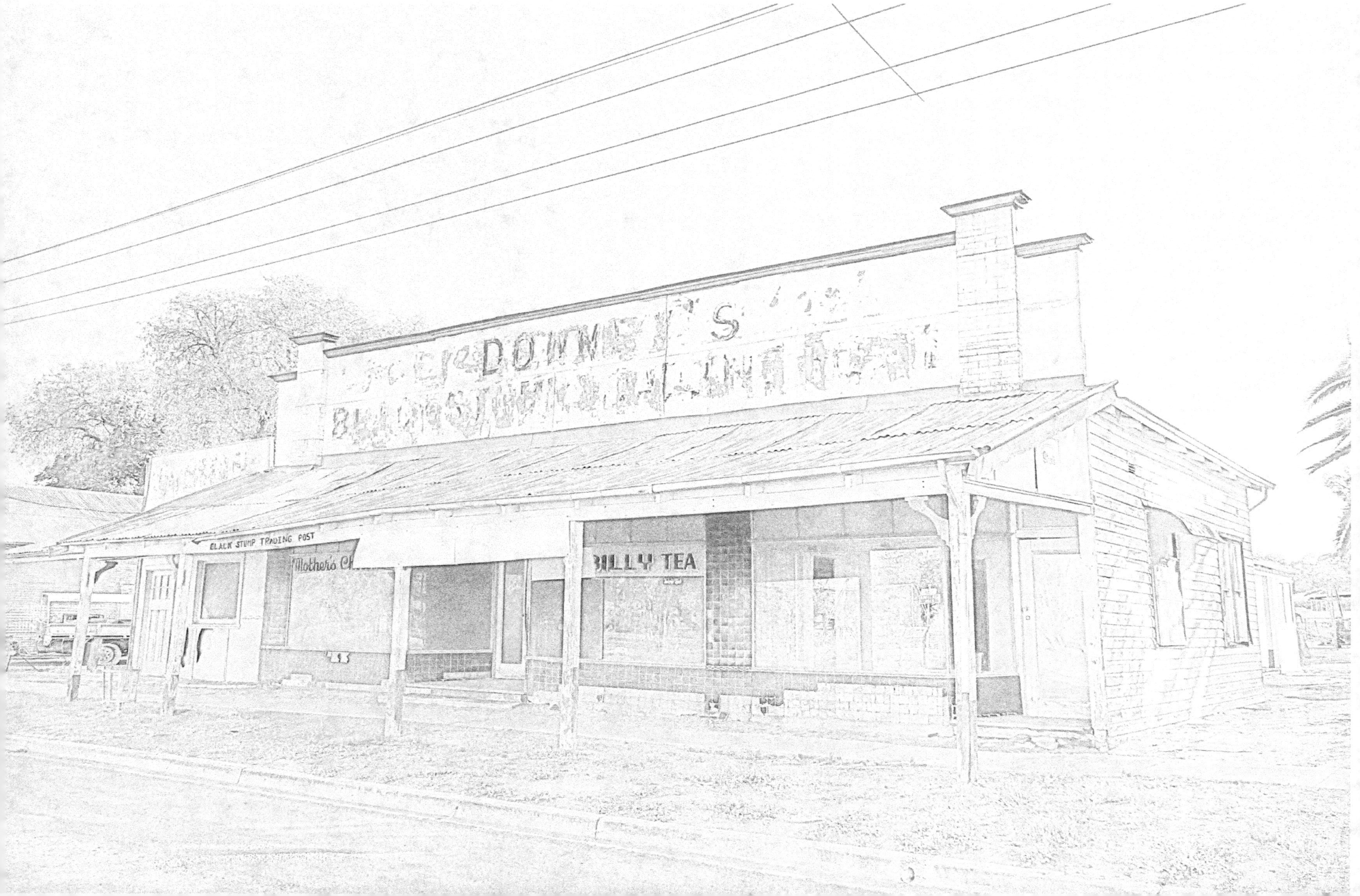
BLACK STUMP TRADING POST
BILLY TEA

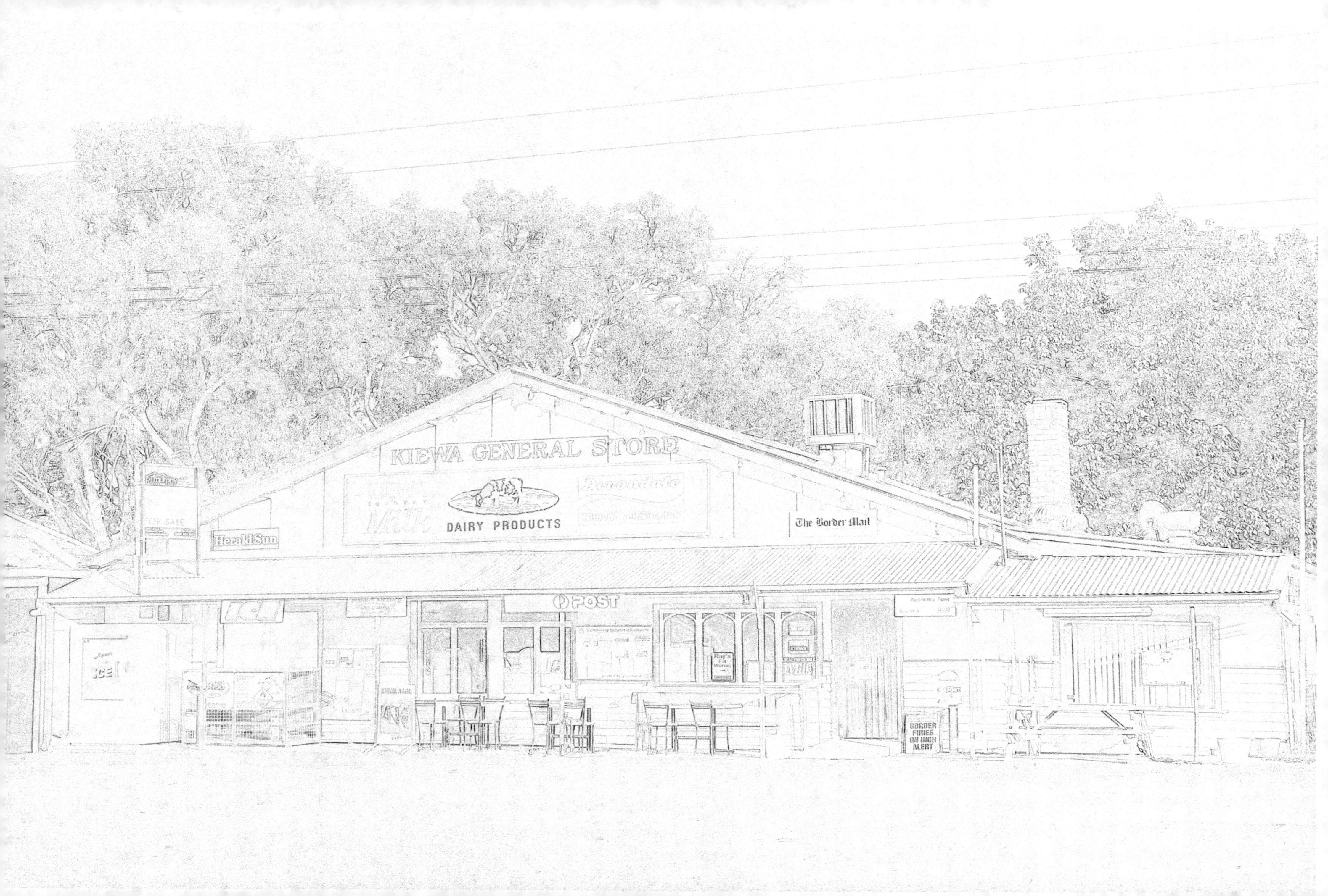
KIEWA GENERAL STORE
DAIRY PRODUCTS
Milk
Herald Sun
The Border Mail
FOR SALE
POST
ICE
Australia Post
BORDER FIRES ON HIGH ALERT

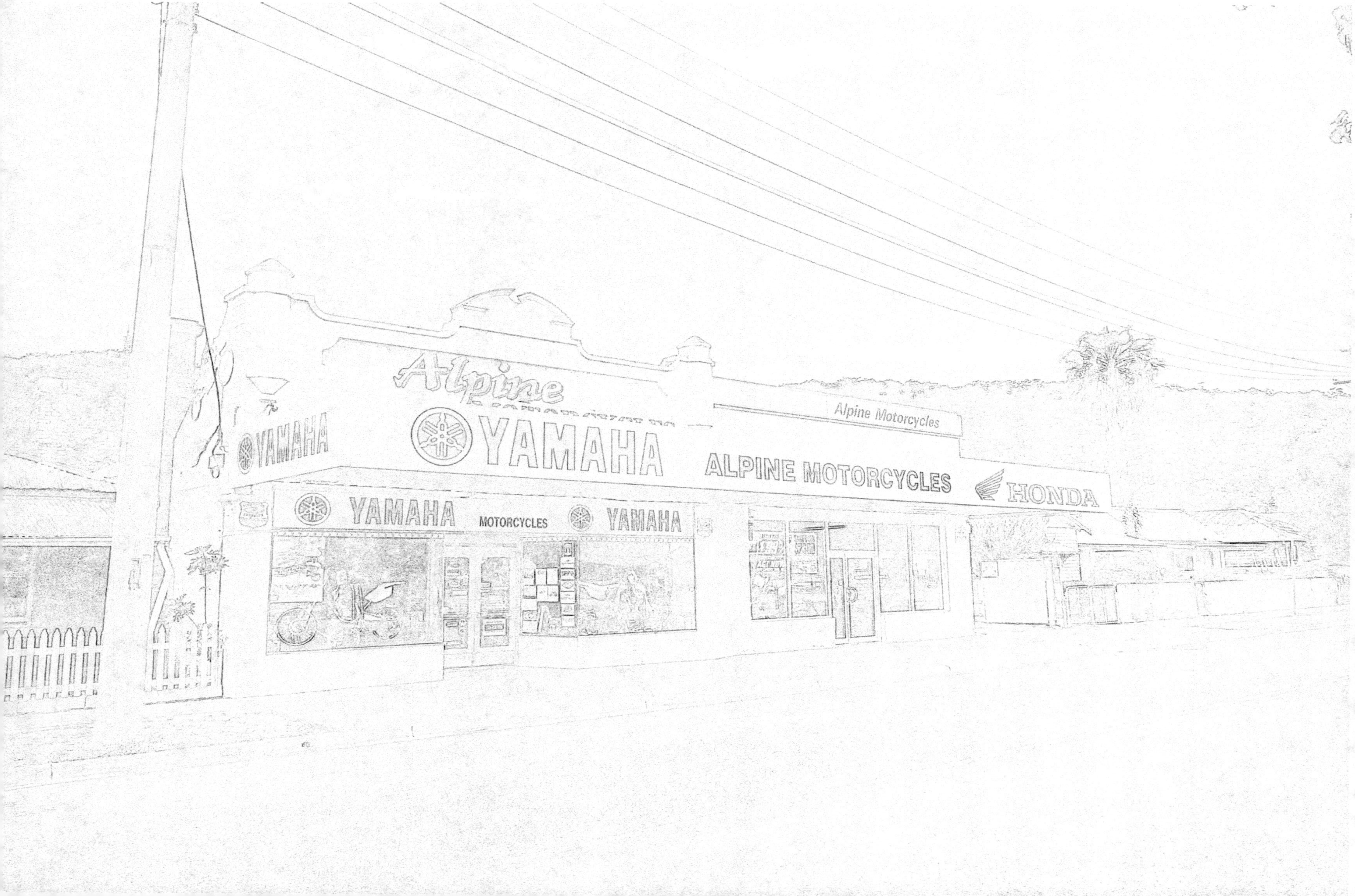
Alpine
YAMAHA
YAMAHA
Alpine Motorcycles
ALPINE MOTORCYCLES
HONDA
YAMAHA
MOTORCYCLES
YAMAHA

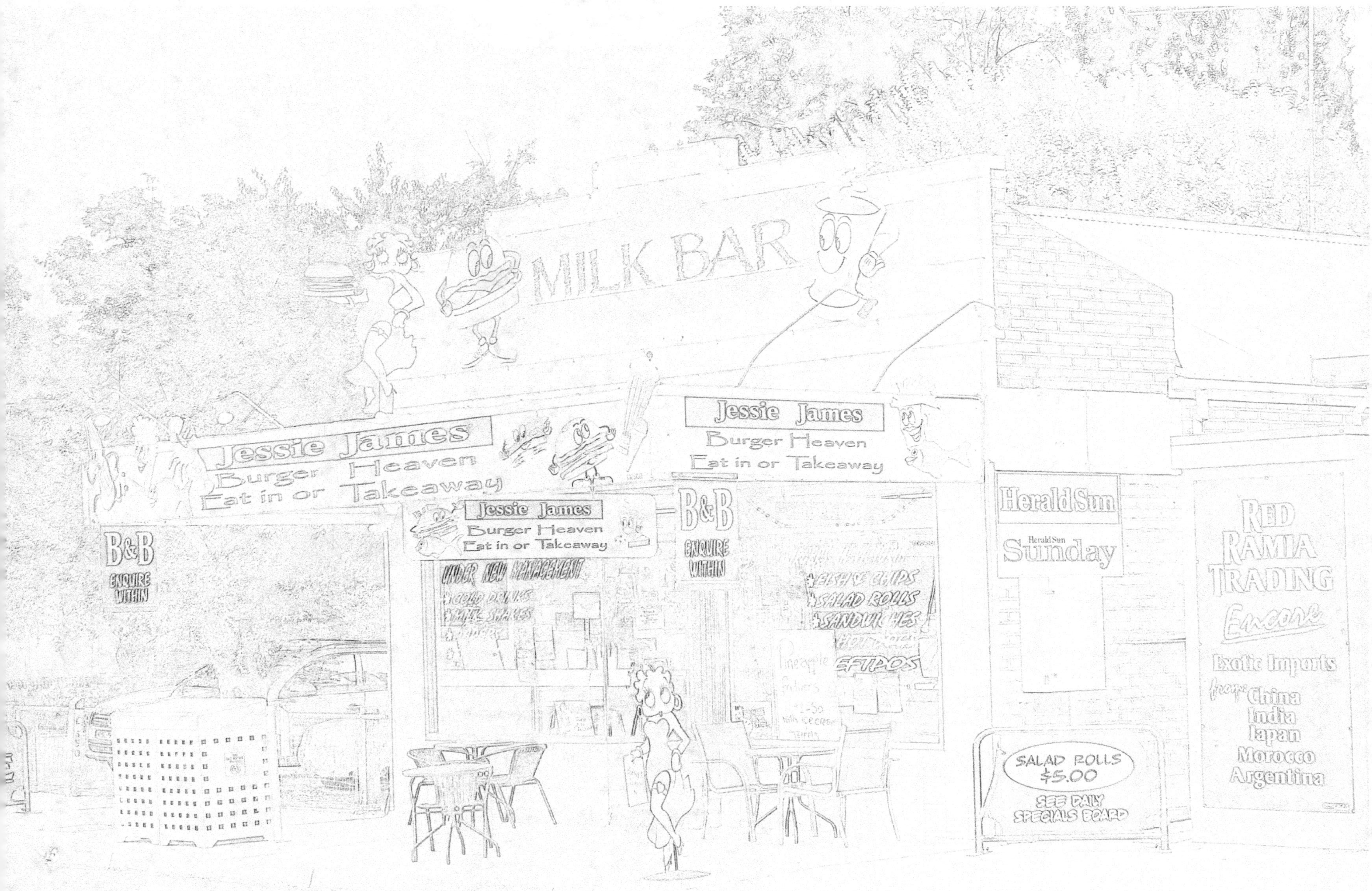
MILK BAR
Jessie James
Burger Heaven
Eat in or Takeaway
B&B
ENQUIRE WITHIN
Jessie James
Burger Heaven
Eat in or Takeaway
UNDER NEW MANAGEMENT
*COLD DRINKS
*MILK SHAKES
Jessie James
Burger Heaven
Eat in or Takeaway
B&B
ENQUIRE WITHIN
*FISH & CHIPS
*SALAD ROLLS
*SANDWICHES
EFTPOS
HeraldSun
Herald Sun
Sunday
SALAD ROLLS
$5.00
SEE DAILY
SPECIALS BOARD
RED
RAMIA
TRADING
Encore
Exotic Imports
from China
India
Japan
Morocco
Argentina

www.ingramcontent.com/pod-product-compliance
Lightning Source LLC
Chambersburg PA
CBHW081050180526
45170CB00005B/1745
9780359820610